Parables of Jesus

Parables of Jesus

John L. McLaughlin

NOVALIS

© 2004 Novalis, Saint Paul University, Ottawa, Canada

Cover: Allegro 168 Inc.

Layout: Christiane Lemire, Francine Petitclerc

Business Office:
Novalis
49 Front Street East, 2nd Floor
Toronto, Ontario, Canada
M5E 1B3
Phone: 1-877-702-7773 or (416) 363-3303
Fax: 1-877-702-7775 or (416) 363-9409
E-mail: cservice@novalis.ca

www.novalis.ca

Library and Archives Canada Cataloguing in Publication

McLaughlin, John L. (John Leo)
     Parables of Jesus / John L. McLaughlin.

ISBN 2-89507-520-4

     1. Jesus Christ–Parables. I. Title.

BT375.3.M24 2004   226.8'06   C2004-904250-5

Printed in Canada.

The Scripture quotations contained herein are from the New Revised Standard Version of the Bible, copyrighted 1989 by the Division of Christian Education of the National Council of the Churches of Christ in the United States of America, and are used by permission. All rights reserved.

We acknowledge the financial support of the Government of Canada through the Book Publishing Industry Development Program (BPIDP) for our publishing activities.

5 4 3 2 1 08 07 06 05 04

NOVALIS

To my colleagues

Contents

Preface 9

1. The Two Builders: "It did not fall."
   (Matthew 7:24-27) 15

2. The Sower: "Yielding thirty and sixty
   and a hundredfold."
   (Mark 4:1-9).. 22

3. The Wheat and the Weeds: "Let both of them
   grow together until the harvest."
   (Matthew 13:24-30) 29

4. The Mustard Seed: "It becomes the greatest
   of all shrubs."
   (Mark 4:30-32).. 35

5. The Lost Sheep: "He rejoices over it more
   than over the ninety-nine."
   (Matthew 18:10-14 / Luke 15:1-7) 40

6. The Unmerciful Slave: "Should you not have
   had mercy on your fellow slave?"
   (Matthew 18:23-35) 47

7. The Good Samaritan: "Who is my neighbour?"
   (Luke 10:25-37) 53

8. The Rich Fool: "This very night your life
   is being demanded of you."
   (Luke 12:16-21) 59

9. The Great Dinner/Banquet: "Bring in the poor,
   the crippled, the blind, and the lame."
   (Luke 14:16-24 and Matthew 22:1-10) 64

10. The Prodigal and His Brother: "He was lost
and has been found."
(Luke 15:11-32) 71

11. The Dishonest Manager: "The children
of this age are more shrewd in dealing
with their own generation than are
the children of light."
(Luke 16:1-8) 77

12. The Widow and the Unjust Judge:
"Will he delay long in helping them?"
(Luke 18:1-8) 82

13. The Pharisee and the Tax Collector:
"This man went down to his home justified."
(Luke 18:9-14) 87

14. The Labourers in the Vineyard: "Am I not
allowed to do what I choose with
what belongs to me?"
(Matthew 20:1-16) 94

15. The Tenants: "What then will the owner
of the vineyard do?"
(Mark 12:1-9)... 101

16. The Talents: "Well done, good
and trustworthy slave."
(Matthew 25:14-30) 108

17. The Sheep and the Goats: "Just as you did it
to one of the least...you did it to me."
(Matthew 25:31-46) 114

Index of Scripture References 120

Preface

"With many such parables he spoke the word to them, as they were able to hear it" (Mark 4:33). This verse summarizes one of Jesus' main methods of communicating his message to the people of his day. The word "parable" is a combination of two Greek words that mean "put (*bolē*) beside (*para*)." Thus, a parable is something that is "put beside" something else. Although by definition a parable is simply any comparison between two things, most of us think of parables more specifically as short, memorable stories that illustrate different elements of Jesus' teaching. Such stories draw a comparison between the reign of God or the Christian life, for instance, and characters and events that Jesus' audience encountered regularly in their own lives.

There are three points to keep in mind when reflecting on the Gospel parables. First, they were addressed to the general population, not a highly educated elite. As such, they were meant to be easily understood, without a detailed explanation. Some parables, such as The Sower or The Wheat and the Weeds, are followed by elaborate allegories, in which each element of the story is said to symbolize something else completely (see Chapters 2 and 3 of this book). But these were probably added later. Second, parables often contain a surprising element. Generally, something in the parable is different from the normal experience, and those who heard the parable would have noticed this "twist" right away. Third, since the parables are found within the Scriptures, they are part of God's Word, which was addressed not only to those who first heard it, but also to us today. The goal of the *Jesus Speaks Today* series is to show how that Word continues to be relevant to our contemporary world while respecting its original context.

This book will focus on the story parables, reflecting on most (but not all) of the parables found in Matthew, Mark and Luke. The approach is the same as in the other three books in this series: my earlier volume, *The Questions of Jesus*; Richard Ascough's *Miracles of Jesus*; and Alicia Batten's forthcoming *Teachings of Jesus*. Each chapter reflects on a single parable, considering what it would have meant for the people who first heard it. After exploring how they would have understood the parable in the light of the First Testament and on the basis of their life within the Roman Empire, we will look at what the parable means for us today.

Some of the words and phrases used in this book may require an explanation. First, traditional terminology for the two main divisions of the Bible is problematic and has implications for how one interprets both sections. "Old Testament" connotes "antiquated," "outdated" and even "replaced" for some. "Hebrew Bible" is popular in many circles, but designating the material by its (primary) language of composition does not take into account the Aramaic portions of Ezra and Daniel or the extensive scholarly use of ancient translations, to say nothing of the second part of the Bible, which still tends to be called the "New Testament." "Hebrew Bible" also does not incorporate the deutero-canonical books, some written exclusively in Greek, which Roman Catholics and Eastern Orthodox Christians consider scriptural but Protestants and Jews do not. Similarly, "Jewish Bible/Scripture" is inadequate for Christians in general, for whom that material is also part of their Scriptures. Therefore, the terms "First Testament" and "Second Testament" are used in this book for the two main divisions of the biblical literature.

Second, in the following pages the phrase "Synoptic Gospels" is used in reference to the Gospels of Matthew, Mark and Luke. These three are called "synoptic" because, in contrast to the Fourth Gospel (John), their presentation of Jesus can be seen (*-optic*) together (*syn-*). If they are arranged in three parallel columns (different editions of such a synopsis have been published), it becomes clear that Matthew, Mark and Luke describe the same basic events from the life of Jesus in roughly the same order and often with the exact same words. This suggests that there is a literary relationship among these three Gospels, such that two of the authors have copied significant portions from one or two of the others. The most commonly accepted solution to this "synoptic problem" is that Matthew and Luke, working independently of each other, followed the narrative outline and content of Mark's Gospel, but also supplemented it with material taken from a collection of Jesus' sayings. This second source is designated with the letter "Q," from the German word *Quelle*, which simply means "source."

Third, LORD is used in place of the name of the God of Israel. Even though the name is present in the ancient Hebrew manuscripts of the First Testament, a growing sense of the sacredness of both God and God's name, plus a concern that one might inadvertently take God's name in vain, eventually led to the practice of not pronouncing the name that was written. Instead, to this day, observant Jews substitute the term *ădōnāy*, which means "my Lord," wherever the name itself appears. In keeping with this practice, the word LORD is used in place of the divine name, but it is written in capital letters to signify that it is the divine name that is meant and not just the noun "lord."

Finally, the abbreviations BCE and CE are used. These stand for "Before the Common Era" and "Common Era," and cover the same period as BC ("Before Christ") and AD ("Anno Domini" = "The Year of the Lord"). BCE and CE are more commonly used by biblical scholars than are BC and AD.

The following chapters each begin with a reference indicating where in the Bible to find the parable being discussed. Reading about the Bible should not take the place of reading the Bible itself, so read each passage before you read the chapter. This book uses the New Revised Standard Version (NRSV) when quoting from the Bible, but any modern translation will do. Differences in wording among translations are usually the result of the different translators' choices as to how to render a word that has more than one nuance. Do not let that interfere with letting the biblical texts come alive for you today, which is the purpose of this book.

Two years ago, I returned to Canada to teach at my alma mater, after seven wonderful years teaching in the United States. Since then, I have had the pleasure and honour to teach alongside some of those who taught me, as well as with a newer generation of scholars. My colleagues in Toronto have created a faith-filled and scholarly environment in which to teach and to continue to learn. This book is dedicated to them.

The fact that Christianity is a fundamentally communal religion is central to this book's content. In keeping with this, it has benefited from the contributions of people too numerous to name. I do wish to acknowledge the particular efforts of some, however. At Novalis, Kevin Burns first suggested developing my earlier book, *The Questions of Jesus*, into the *Jesus Speaks Today* series and has skillfully guided that larger project and its individual components ever since. Anne Louise Mahoney has been a wonderful editor, catching errors and suggesting countless improvements. Mark Yenson, a doctoral student at St. Michael's who has been my research assistant, proofread various drafts of the manuscript and compiled the Index of Scripture References.

John L. McLaughlin
Faculty of Theology
University of St. Michael's College
July 2004

1

The Two Builders

"It did not fall."
Matthew 7:24-27

There are two seasons in Israel. From May to September it is hot and dry, with virtually no rain. During this period, the water reserves that people have stored up decrease, the level of lakes and rivers drops, and most of the smaller creeks and streams dry up completely. These dried-up streams are called *wadis*; one can see the channel made by flowing water, but the water itself no longer flows. In contrast, the rainy season spans October to April. During these months most of the annual rainfall, and occasionally snowfall, occurs. In the central mountains, as much as 100 cm (40 inches) of rain can fall during these months. These levels can become dangerous during the middle of the rainy season, since about 70 per cent of the annual rainfall occurs between November and February. During this period, sudden, intense rain in the mountains is quickly funnelled along the rocky surface, collecting in valleys as it goes along and often creating flash floods through the previously dry *wadis*. Moreover, these floods can be made worse by storm winds blowing in from the Mediterranean Sea.

That is the background for this parable about two builders who each built a house, one on rock and one on sand. When the harsh winter weather arrived, the first house survived because it had been built on stone, above the flood level, where its foundation could not be weakened by the raging water. This in turn meant that it was better able to withstand the rain and stormy winds that accompanied the flooding. It is no wonder Jesus called the first builder "wise," since he built his house in a way that allowed it to withstand the elements.

In contrast, the "foolish" man built his house on sand. This suggests two possible locations in Israel. The first is along the coast. In Israel the shore of the Mediterranean Sea consists primarily of sandy beaches. In the dry summer season, they look lovely, and therefore seem to be a perfect spot for a house. But when the winter wind and rain arrive, the region is much less pleasant, especially if a storm from the Mediterranean brings large waves along with the wind and rain.

The other possible location for a house built upon sand is in one of the dried-up *wadis*. To someone who is new to the region or who is simply "foolish," this, too, would look like a pleasant spot for a house, with soft sand and gentle slopes to provide protection from the elements. But if a flash flood came racing along the *wadi*, it would instantly sweep away any building in its path. Since the parable contrasts the one who is "wise" with the one who is "foolish," a *wadi* seems the more likely spot for the house built on sand. It emphasizes the second builder's failure to act upon what those around him knew, and the result makes him look ridiculous.

Jesus links this contrast between the wise and foolish with his Sermon on the Mount, which comes just before this parable (Matthew 5–7). Specifically, the wise builder is like someone who does not just hear the Sermon but acts upon it. In contrast, the foolish builder hears Jesus' words, but fails to put them into practice.

The Sermon on the Mount contains some of Jesus' most famous teachings. It includes the Beatitudes, the Lord's Prayer, teachings about trusting God, the relative value of wealth, the need to turn the other cheek and many others. These teachings are central to living the Christian life. In fact, the Sermon on the Mount has been described as the first Christian catechism, because it puts forward Jesus' vision of how people are meant to live in relationship to God and one another. So, within the Sermon we find concrete instructions concerning what it means to live under the reign of God.

The concept of the reign of God was central to Jesus' life and teaching. Jesus began his preaching ministry by announcing, "The time is fulfilled, and the kingdom of God has come near" (Mark 1:15). Although the phrase is often translated as the "kingdom" of God, "kingship" or "reign" not only reflects the original Greek more accurately, it emphasizes that this is a form of social organization in which God's will for humankind is actively put into practice. God's reign is a concrete alternative to every political "kingdom" on earth, both past and present. It is a society in which God's love and concern for every single human being is embodied in every member of that society. In short, the reign of God means establishing a new way of life. The Sermon on the Mount gives some very specific guidelines for how to accomplish that.

The reign of God means a world that is very different from the one in which Jesus and his followers lived: the Roman Empire. For that reason, most of what Jesus said went against the social norms of his day. The Beatitudes, for example, show preference for the weaker members of society, not the strong as was the custom. For example, Jesus' advice that his followers should go a second mile if forced to go one mile (Matthew 5:41) is not about serving others. Roman soldiers were allowed to force local inhabitants to carry their gear for one mile, but no further. Thus, carrying a Roman's gear for two miles would get the soldier into trouble. Jesus was actually urging people to use the Roman system of oppression against itself. Similarly, when Jesus tells us to "turn the other cheek" (Matthew 5:39) he is not encouraging passive acceptance of violence. In Matthew he speaks specifically of someone hitting you on the right cheek. For a right-handed person (as the majority are) to hit someone on the right cheek requires a backhanded slap, which was the type of blow used by a superior towards an inferior person. By turning the other (left) cheek, you would force the person to hit you with an open hand, which implied equality in that culture. In Jesus' day, turning the other cheek meant refusing to accept the role of an inferior and insisting on being treated as an equal. This is a far cry from being passive, and yet it also avoids responding to violence with violence.

When people of that time put Jesus' teachings in the Sermon on the Mount into effect, the result was a society very different from that of the dominant Roman Empire, which then included much of the known world. Creating a new society in the face of such great power and control required more than just thinking about it. As Jesus said, it was not enough to agree with his ideas and hope they might come to pass; people must also act upon them (see Luke 6:46). Only when people begin to live as Jesus taught do relationships change and people begin to treat each other differently. Once that new community starts to take root, it will form a support system for others who are trying to live differently, showing concretely that it can be done, and reinforcing the intentions of those who are trying to do so.

By living out Jesus' teachings together with other believers, we create an alternative society that reinforces our efforts to build that society. Moreover, it provides us with a solid foundation from which to respond and resist when opposition comes. In the same way that a house built upon rock is less likely to be affected by sudden floods and the harsh weather of the rainy season, so, too, those who have established a community with like-minded individuals will be able to stand firm against opposition. This opposition may come in the form of ridicule for daring to be different, or outright persecution from those who feel threatened by people who have chosen another way to live. Nonetheless, when Christians live the way that Jesus calls for, even when it is difficult, they know that they are not alone.

If that is not motivation enough, one need only recall what Jesus said immediately before this parable: "Not everyone who says to me 'Lord, Lord,' will enter the kingdom of heaven, but only the one who does the will of my Father in heaven" (Matthew 7:21). He went on to say that not even working miracles, performing exorcisms or speaking prophecies is enough. As this parable illustrates, what is essential is acting upon his words. Jesus came to teach us how to establish the reign of God here on earth, which requires that we come together as a community of faithful believers who live out his teaching in order to create a new community of love for one another. Although mighty deeds of power may seem impressive, they are not central to God's reign. The kind of lifestyle rooted in the Sermon on the Mount is.

Our contemporary society is a little different from the Roman Empire. The way we hit other people does not have the same significance as it did then, and the places where soldiers can force civilians to carry their luggage are (thankfully) much fewer. But that does not mean our society automatically meets God's plans for humankind. We must constantly ask ourselves whether we have yet embodied the community Jesus outlined 2000 years ago. An honest evaluation will lead us to answer "no." But that should not lead to despair. It is never too late to relocate our house to solid rock. All we have to do is think about how Jesus asks each of us to transform our world and do it. Everyone who does so will be a wise builder, not a foolish one.

2

The Sower

"Yielding thirty and sixty and a
hundredfold."
Mark 4:1-9

Farming practices in Israel during the time of Jesus were very different from those in North America today. Modern farms are often large operations that occupy vast amounts of land. By contrast, in first-century Israel, most farming was done by individuals on small parcels of land, because most farming was done in order to grow the food people needed to feed their families. If there happened to be a particularly good harvest one year the extra crops might be sold or traded, but that was more often the exception than the rule.

The much smaller size of ancient farms provided the context for the second major difference between ancient and modern farming practices. Whereas today's farmers have the advantage of machinery to till the earth and plant the seed, the small-scale farmer of Jesus' day sowed the seed by hand. The farmer would simply walk across his field and scatter the seed, throwing it on either side as he walked. Only after the seed was sown was the field plowed, thereby turning the seed under the soil itself.

This helps to explain many of the features of this parable, starting with the various places where some seeds fall, namely "on the path," "on rocky ground" and "among thorns." Mark does not say that large amounts of seed fell in each of these places. Rather, the original Greek mentions "one," then "another" and then "another." This means that most modern translations ("some seed" followed by "others") are slightly misleading. The parable does not describe someone indiscriminately throwing seed around in the hopes that it might happen to land on good soil and grow into mature plants. Such a farmer would probably not have much of a harvest, and would be unlikely to survive many years if he kept planting crops that way. Instead, even though the sower sows the seed by scattering it, he intends for it to land on the good soil. It is simply an unfortunate accident that a few individual seeds land elsewhere and for different reasons do not bear fruit.

The first place a seed goes astray is on the path. This might refer to a main road running alongside the field, but it more likely means a path for walking between fields. In either case, the result is the same. Since the path would have been packed down from travel, the seed lay exposed and was easily consumed by the birds seeking food. Another seed fell on rocky ground. The first thing that comes to mind when we hear this is an area littered with stones, but Mark specifies that "it did not have much soil." This is a place where the bedrock is close to the surface and there is very little topsoil. As a result, the soil did not hold much moisture, which was essential in a hot, arid land like Israel. So, although the seed was able to sprout, its roots could not go deep enough to reach the underground water sources, and the plant withered under the scorching Mediterranean sun. The third place where a seed landed was among thorns, which competed with the plant for both moisture and sunlight, eventually choking it so that it died.

But what happened to the few seeds that went astray is not the main point of this parable. The sower's purpose was to sow seed in good soil – soil that was deep enough to retain some moisture, which would allow the seeds to take root, gain nourishment from the ground and grow into mature plants. And that is exactly what happened to most of the seed. Earlier Mark mentioned only single seeds on the path, on rocky ground and among the thorns, but in verse 8 the Greek switches from the singular word "another" to the plural term "others." Not only do most of the seeds bear fruit, Mark even says that the seed that fell into good soil yielded "thirty and sixty and a hundredfold." This does not mean that each seed yielded that many plants, however; for Mark, this phrase is cumulative. A thirty-fold harvest would be great indeed, and one that was sixty-fold greater still. So how much more fantastic would a hundredfold harvest be! In keeping with comparable Semitic expressions (cf. Amos 1–2), it is the final number in the sequence that is important. The others are given first in order to emphasize the final one.

So what is the message of the parable of The Sower? Unfortunately, Jesus does not provide a point of comparison as he does so often elsewhere. He does not begin by saying, "The kingdom is like..." or "The Father is like...." However, a few verses later we do find an interpretation of the parable in the form of an allegory, in which every element of the parable is said to symbolize something else. Thus, in Mark 4:13-20 we are told that the seed is the word of God; the birds who eat the seed along the path stand for Satan, who immediately deceives some who hear the word; the rocky ground represents persecution, which cause others to fall away; and the thorns stand for the cares of the world that prevent still others from following the gospel. The good soil symbolizes those who accept the gospel message and bear great fruit as a result. This section does not identify the sower, but he probably stands for either Jesus or his followers, who imitate Jesus in spreading the gospel message.

This allegory is very well known and at first glance appears to make sense in this context. However, most scholars think this interpretation was developed some time after the parable was first told. To begin with, as I pointed out in the Preface, the parables are simple stories intended to make a single point without elaborate explanations. Thus, at the end of the parable Jesus says, "Let anyone with ears to hear listen!" (v. 9); the implication is that people should be able to understand the message without needing to have it explained to them. Also, the explanation is given three verses after the parable ends, and only to the disciples. This does not fit with Jesus' proclamation that people should hear and respond to the parable. There are other inconsistencies as well. For instance, in the interpretation numerous seeds go astray in each place, representing groups of people, but in the parable only a single seed fell in each of the three areas. Moreover, the allegorical interpretation itself is not consistent: verse 14 says that the seed is the Word, but in the following verses the seed stands for various groups of people who hear that Word. All of these points indicate that the allegorical interpretation was added later.

If we want to know the meaning of the parable as it was originally told, therefore, we should look at the content of the parable itself. The parable does not emphasize the sower's actions in sowing the seed, but merely describes this in passing, without providing much detail. The fact that he sowed his seed is the basis for the parable – if he did not sow his seeds, there would not even be a story to tell – but not the main point. Nor is the point what happens to a few individual seeds that do not land where the sower intended. Although their fate is presented in a bit more detail, that is done only to provide a contrast for what happens to most of the seed. The main point of the parable is that the seed that lands on good soil yields an abundant harvest, much greater than one would expect.

What is lacking in the parable is a point of comparison to understand the significance of this great harvest. Instead, the reader is expected to provide one. This parable forces us to ask, "What does this mean for me?" There are at least three answers to this question, depending on the audience.

For the crowds listening to Jesus tell this parable, the point of comparison was probably Jesus' own ministry. They could see with their own eyes how people responded to this man's preaching. The very fact that crowds were attracted to him and his message indicates that he was bearing fruit among them. This would have been surprising to many in light of his place of origin, since even one of his own disciples once asked, "Can anything good come out of Nazareth?" (John 1:46). Galilee was an insignificant part of a small corner of the Roman Empire, yet here was one of its citizens preaching with confidence and healing the sick. The results were there for all to see.

For Mark's community, who came to know Jesus through Mark's Gospel, the message would have been about the spread of the early Christian community. Despite some problems along the way, 40 years after Jesus' death his followers were spreading throughout the Roman Empire, and in the case of Mark's own group, had put down roots in Rome itself. Many would have considered this an astonishing development for a movement that began in an unsophisticated and unimportant area on the fringes of the Empire.

And what does it mean for us hearing or reading it today? It invites us to focus on what is dramatic and surprising about living as a Christian today. The North American context is vastly different from that of the audiences of Jesus or Mark. Here, Christianity is the majority religion and few of us face explicit persecution. But that in itself could create a problem, for we might become complacent, with the result that others no longer see Christ reflected in our lives. Where that is the case, it may be surprising that some people still seek to live out the radical life of love to which Jesus calls his followers and often succeed beyond all imagining. People such as Mother Teresa or Jean Vanier, who have given their lives in service to people who are poor, who are dying or who have disabilities often inspire others to do likewise, resulting in a much greater harvest than one would expect from the life of a single person. They yield "thirty and sixty and a hundredfold."

3

The Wheat and the Weeds

"Let both of them grow together
until the harvest."
Matthew 13:24-30

The parable of The Wheat and the Weeds is found only in Matthew's Gospel, where it appears between the parable of The Sower and the parable of The Mustard Seed. The result is a series of parables dealing with agricultural matters in general and with seeds in particular. Thus, we once again encounter a story of a man sowing seeds in his field, but this time the point is that both good and bad seeds are sometimes found together in a single field.

This situation was not intentional, however. It is stressed at the beginning that this individual sowed "good seed." Unfortunately, during the night an enemy sneaked into the field and planted weeds among the good seeds. The enemy's actions were not revealed until the two types of plants began to grow, and it became obvious that there were weeds growing among the wheat that the sower had planted. The man's slaves wanted to pull up the weeds, but he would not allow them to, for two reasons. First, they might not always be able to distinguish young weeds from young wheat. Second, since the roots of both plants were competing for the same soil, by pulling up the weeds they might accidentally uproot some of the wheat as well, losing some, if not all, of the crop in the process. Instead, the owner decided to wait until the harvest, at which time the two kinds of plants could be safely separated, with the wheat stored for future use while the weeds are burned as rubbish.

Like the parable of The Sower, this story has an allegorical interpretation linked to it. But again, the explanation is separated from the story itself, this time by six verses. In Matthew's Gospel, we meet the parables of The Mustard Seed and The Yeast, plus a statement summarizing how and why Jesus taught in parables, before we reach the explanation of the parable of The Wheat and the Weeds (Matthew 13:36-43). The explanation makes a direct connection between elements of the parable and things outside the story: "The one who sows the good seed is the Son of Man; the field is the world, and the good seed are the children of the kingdom; the weeds are the children of the evil one, and the enemy who sowed them is the devil; the harvest is the end of the age, and the reapers are angels. Just as the weeds are collected and burned up with fire, so will it be at the end of the age" (Matthew 13:37-40).

Once again, the distance between the parable and the allegorical interpretation suggests that this interpretation developed later. However, there is some basis for the general thrust of the interpretation. A harvest was a common metaphor for the last judgment in the Scriptures (e.g., Isaiah 17:1-11; Jeremiah 51:33; Matthew 9:37-38). In keeping with this metaphor, the distinction between wheat and weeds easily lends itself to the idea of good and bad people who will be judged, and the reference to an enemy would lead most people to think of The Enemy: Satan.

Nonetheless, it is possible to get the point of the parable without the explanation in Matthew (3:37-40). For instance, in the parable the one who sows the weeds is simply called "an enemy." He is not identified as "*the* enemy" or even "the man's enemy." When the slaves bring the news to the householder's attention, he does not suggest that it was done by anyone specific, such as "my enemy," but refers to the person in general terms. In other words, he has no idea who this person is; his exact identity is secondary to the parable. The enemy's only function in the story is to sow weeds among the wheat, and we don't need to know anything more about him than that. Nor is he punished at the end, since he is unknown. What matters is the result of his actions: the growing weeds and their ultimate fate.

And yet, the parable does have a future orientation, because it deals with planting and harvesting. One sows in the hope that the seeds will survive, will develop into healthy plants and, in the case of crops like wheat, will be used for food. But plants don't grow overnight, and if we harvest food plants too soon, they will not be ripe and therefore unfit for human consumption; or, if they are edible, the yield will be reduced. So one of the lessons we can draw from this parable is the need for patience. The slaves wanted to pull up the weeds as soon as they were discovered, but the owner was wiser and ordered them to be left until the wheat had matured. Likewise, we should not rush to act, especially in a situation that calls for discernment in distinguishing between what is good and bad. The difference may not always be immediately evident, and even when it is, we still need to ask whether eliminating what is bad might harm what is good. In some cases, it is best to leave the separation until later or, better still, leave it to God.

This interpretation touches on a second point we can draw from the parable of The Wheat and the Weeds. Life is not black and white; rather, it is usually quite complex. Most situations are not all good or all bad, but a mixture of the two. For the early church, this parable was a reminder that even the assembly of believers was not perfect. They were a mixed group of people with different abilities and different levels of development. This is nowhere more evident than in Paul's First Letter to the Corinthians. Paul spends much of the letter correcting that community for their shortcomings, which included misunderstanding the Gospel message and the nature of Christian life together, and fighting over whom they considered their leader (see 1 Corinthians 3:4-6).

Things are not all that different today. Our own Christian gatherings include a mix of people of different nationalities and races, reflecting a range in levels of education, wealth, intelligence and ability. What's more, people are at different stages of spiritual or moral development. When many people are involved, there are going to be differences and challenges. This parable encourages us to accept this fact. It is human nature to be less than perfect, which is why God offered us salvation in the first place. As long as our churches are made up of human beings, they will be imperfect. As one anonymous wise person once said, "If you find a perfect church, don't join it, because you'll ruin it."

This parable also encourages us not to be too quick to judge others by appearances. The owner told the slaves not to pluck the weeds, because they might not be able to distinguish them from the wheat, and because even if they could they might pull up the wheat in the process. We, too, may not always be as insightful as we think. There is often more going on inside a person than what we see on the surface. It is a cliché that only God knows what is in a person's heart, but it is also true. People who look like weeds to us may not be. On the other hand, those who appear to be good and righteous may not be either. We should think long and hard before drawing conclusions about others.

There is one other point to draw from this parable. I noted above that the enemy in this story is purposely left unidentified, and the owner himself doesn't blame a specific opponent for the weeds in his field. This warns us not to assume that we will always know the source of the trouble in our lives. At times it may be obvious, but sometimes we won't recognize the source of the "weeds" among us. Even though we cannot always eliminate them once they've been sown, we should still be on our guard for bad seeds before they have a chance to take root and grow.

4

The Mustard Seed

"It becomes the greatest of all shrubs."
Mark 4:30-32

The point of comparison in this parable is clear from the very beginning, when Jesus asks, "With what can we compare the kingdom of God, or what parable will we use for it?" He then introduces the image of the mustard seed. However, it is not just the mustard seed itself that is at issue, but rather the entire span of its development into a mature plant. If the point of the parable was simply that birds were able to nest under very large branches, then many other seeds would have sufficed. Jesus specifies that it is a mustard seed, which is tiny; we must consider this when we interpret the parable's meaning.

The mustard seed is sown "upon" the ground, not in it, in keeping with the customary means of sowing seeds in the ancient Near East (see Chapter 2 of this book). For Mark, this is not a cultivated field (as in Matthew 13:31) or a garden (as in Luke 13:19), but simply open ground. This may reflect Mark's desire to stress that humans are not able to plan the development of the kingdom, which we will see is a major part of the parable's message.

A central element of the parable is the emphasis on the size of both the seed and the plant that results. According to Mark, the mustard seed, which "is the smallest of all the seeds on earth," becomes "the greatest of all shrubs." Neither statement, however, is correct. While the mustard seed is indeed small, it is not the tiniest one that exists, neither the smallest known seed nor even the smallest seed that was planted in those days. Still, it was a common image for the smallest thing imaginable. For instance, Matthew 17:20 and Luke 17:6 use the mustard seed to indicate that even the smallest amount of faith could move a mountain; the rabbis also used the mustard seed in their proverbial sayings to represent the smallest possible amount. And even though a mature mustard plant could reach a height of 3 metres (10 feet), other shrubs were larger. Still, the point of the parable is not to teach botany, but to compare the smallness of the seed to the greatness of the resulting plant.

Put another way, the kingdom of God has its beginnings in the smallest, least likely sources, and yet becomes very large. The mustard plant becomes so big that "the birds of the air can make nests in its shade"; this alludes to a number of texts from the First Testament in which large trees symbolize great nations under the authority of God. For instance, Ezekiel uses the majestic cedar of Lebanon to represent the restored nations of

Israel (17:22-23) and Assyria (31:6). In the first passage, birds live under it and "in the shade of its branches will nest" (unlike the Hebrew and NRSV, the ancient Greek translation of this phrase matches Mark's wording exactly) while in the second passage the birds nest in, not under, the cedar's branches (see also Psalm 104:16-17) and animals give birth under it. Similarly, Daniel 4:20-21 describes a massive tree reaching up to heaven that provided nourishment for all, shelter beneath it for the animals and a nesting place for birds in its branches.

However, the mustard plant's branches are not strong enough to support the weight of a bird's nest, which makes the connection with these First Testament texts (except Ezekiel 17:22-23) less than accurate. Matthew and Luke strengthen the link with these texts by saying, incorrectly, that the seed becomes a tree, and that the birds nest in its branches. But since the mustard plant is not a tree, none of these texts, not even Ezekiel, reflects Mark's version of the parable exactly. The fact that Mark alludes to these First Testament texts without calling the mustard plant a tree means he had a reason for choosing "shrub" over "tree." By referring to those texts but not making an exact correlation with them, he indicates that the kingdom is really not like that. The image he gives offers a contrasting image of the kingdom.

As an image for the kingdom, the tiny mustard seed is unexpected. One anticipates a clear expression of the kingdom's greatness in the mature plant, but that expectation is not met. Although the maturing seed "puts forth large branches," it fails to become the magnificent tree that so often served as a symbol of God's reign. The parable thus reverses the expectations that most of Jesus' audience had about the reign of God. It neither begins nor ends in majesty, but at all times exists in a less obvious form than people, both past and present, might expect. As a result, the parable challenges us to seek a new understanding of what the kingdom is really like.

The true nature of God's reign is a matter of humble beginnings and equally humble, although extensive, results. The parable asserts that the kingdom will become great in size but not in (worldly) importance. Once again, the mustard seed is a good choice to make this point, since it was notorious for its rapid growth as well as for its ability to resist efforts to eliminate it. For instance, the Roman historian Pliny noted that once mustard had been introduced into a field, it was almost impossible to get rid of it. In the same way, the kingdom will grow and spread, but those expecting something great and majestic like the cedar tree will be disappointed. The kingdom will increase in size, but instead of a cedar it will be like the mustard plant, big enough to shelter birds but not overly impressive. People who imagine it to be like a cedar – both those who follow Jesus and those who do not – may not even recognize the kingdom, because it will not match their expectations.

This message remains relevant for believers today. It is easy to identify the kingdom in terms of size and power, to think that the community God desires is present when the Church (and churches) are big and powerful. But the parable of The Mustard Seed calls us to reconsider this idea, and to question whether we may at times be trying to become more like a cedar tree than a mustard plant. At the same time, the parable can challenge us to look for the kingdom in unlikely places, represented by groups we might not expect, such as those doing good things out of the public eye, for instance. Many small, humble, often unnoticed organizations or groups inspired by the gospel message work away from the spotlight, spreading God's love embodied in Jesus Christ to those around them. They attract little attention, and even if they do grow in size, they still remain true to their humble origins. We should look to them for a model of the reign of God.

⊗ Ground elder!

5

The Lost Sheep

"He rejoices over it more than over
the ninety-nine."
Matthew 18:10-14 / Luke 15:1-7

The parable of The Lost Sheep is found in both Matthew and Luke, but not in Mark. This means that they derived it from their other source, the Q document (see the Preface). However, the parable occurs in different contexts in the two Gospels, and each contains slightly different details that produce different emphases. Each Gospel even includes a brief, but different, one-sentence interpretative statement, much like the moral we find at the end of one of Aesop's fables. In light of these divergences, it is worth considering both versions to see what insights they provide.

First, let us review the basic story as found in both Matthew and Luke. Someone has a hundred sheep to care for. When he realizes that one of them is missing, he immediately leaves the other 99 and goes in search of it. When he finds it, he rejoices more over it than over the other 99 together.

This is a fairly simple, straightforward story, except for one thing: the shepherd leaves the 99 sheep alone while he searches for the other one. That is not a normal thing to do, which is one of the points of the story. In the ancient world, a shepherd was solely responsible for his flock. The First Testament even mandates the process by which a shepherd can prove that a missing animal was taken by a predator (Exodus 22:10-13; cf. Genesis 31:39; Amos 3:12). So a shepherd had a motive for finding a missing sheep, but leaving the other 99 risks losing them all. The text does not say that he put them in a pen or a cave, or entrusted them to the care of another shepherd, for this would be contrary to the thrust of the parable. The story highlights the shepherd's extravagant action in order to stress the importance of a single animal. In reality, one sheep out of a hundred might be considered an acceptable loss. It was not important enough to risk the entire flock. So by taking that risk, the shepherd shows his great care and concern for the sheep itself, beyond any financial considerations.

In ancient times, the shepherd was a common metaphor for the king caring for his people. Such extreme behaviour on the shepherd's part, however, is probably meant to go beyond that idea to First Testament texts that describe God as the Shepherd of Israel (e.g., Psalm 77:20 and Isaiah 40:11).

In Matthew such associations are strengthened by the statement that the one sheep had "gone astray" (Luke only says "lost"). Probably the most famous reference to straying sheep is Isaiah 53:6, which says, "All we like sheep have gone astray." Straying sheep were also often linked to the failure of Israel's leaders to fulfill their role properly. For instance, Jeremiah says that the shepherds have led the people astray (Jeremiah 50:6; cf. 23:1-4). An even more direct link to Matthew's version of this parable can be found in Ezekiel 34:4 and 11. In verse 4 the prophet condemns the "shepherds of Israel" because they have not brought back those who have strayed, while in verse 11 the LORD says, "I myself will search for my sheep." This is significant: in Matthew, the shepherd goes "in search" (note that the same verb is used) of the stray sheep, whereas in Luke he simply "goes after" the lost sheep. Another relevant difference between the two accounts is where the shepherd leaves the 99 sheep. In Matthew they are on the mountains, while in Luke they are in the wilderness. Once again, Matthew's location echoes First Testament texts, where Israel is described as sheep on a mountain (e.g., 1 Kings 22:17; Jeremiah 50:6 and especially Ezekiel 34:6).

Two final differences exist between the two versions of the parable. The first is how the shepherd reacts to finding the missing sheep. In Matthew he "rejoices over it more than over the ninety-nine that never went astray." His reaction takes place in private; no one else is present. In Luke, however, he goes home and calls together his neighbours to share in his joy. The second difference is the "moral" of the story. Matthew concludes, "It is not the will of your Father in heaven that one of these little ones should be lost," but Luke says, "There will be more joy in heaven over one sinner who repents than over ninety-nine righteous people who need no repentance."

Most of the differences between the two Gospels can be explained in light of either the author's audience or the location of the story within each Gospel. Matthew's community, composed primarily of Jewish-Christians, would have recognized the allusions to the First Testament: the "mountain," the sheep going "astray" and the shepherd going to "search" for it. But these references would have been lost on Luke's Gentile (non-Jewish) audience, so instead Luke refers to the "wilderness," which was more relevant to them. Although the Judean wilderness was hilly, in the larger Roman Empire, "wilderness" had negative connotations. People believed that wild things and even demons lived there. This reflected the fact that the wilderness was on the fringes of the Empire itself, a place from which barbarian tribes attacked civilization.

Where each evangelist placed the story in his Gospel is also significant. Matthew 18 is a "church manual" of sorts, presenting various teachings on the nature of Christian communal life. (In fact, Matthew 18:15 and 17 are two of only three places in all four Gospels where the Greek word for "church" occurs; the other is Matthew 16:18.) Just before this parable, we read in Matthew's Gospel that a child is the greatest in the kingdom, followed by a warning not to cause any of the "little ones" to stumble. After the parable we find procedures for correcting a believer who has sinned (Matthew 18:15-17), a teaching on how frequently one must forgive (77 times; Matthew 18:21-22), and the parable of The Unmerciful Slave (Matthew 18:23-35; see Chapter 6 of this book).

The parable of The Lost Sheep is consistent with the rest of this chapter in Matthew. This story about a shepherd fits with the general guidelines for the community that are found there. Just as when the community calls back someone who has sinned it is to make the first attempts individually and in private, so too the shepherd rejoices privately when he finds the sheep that has strayed; to have a public celebration like in Luke would contradict the procedure for reconciliation. Also, since God has a special concern that members of the community should not cause the "little ones" to go astray, so too Matthew concludes that "it is not the will of your Father in heaven that one of these little ones should be lost."

On the other hand, in Luke's Gospel Jesus tells this parable in response to the Pharisees' and scribes' complaints that he was eating with sinners. In the ancient world, a common way of dealing with those who offended society was to exclude them, a practice we often continue today. In contrast, eating with someone was a way to express solidarity with them. By eating with sinners, Jesus was symbolically welcoming them back into society – the society he was trying to establish, which he called the reign of God. In other words, Jesus wasn't simply breaking the rules; he was breaking down the way the ancient social order itself was structured.

In response to his opponents' complaint, Jesus addressed the parable directly to them, saying, "Which one of you…?" Moreover, he proposed a situation in which one of them loses a sheep. While there is no implication that the hypothetical person has done anything wrong to deserve the loss, the wording still makes it his responsibility. Even if the Pharisees and scribes did not cause the sinners to be lost, sinners are still part of their flock and they have a responsibility to "go after" them. Once the sheep is found, the shepherd throws a party to celebrate finding "my sheep that was lost." Not only does this statement emphasize the fact that the sheep belongs to the shepherd, who has been identified with those complaining about Jesus' table fellowship, but its return is publicly celebrated. The meaning is clear: those who complain about the sinners have a responsibility to seek them out and restore them to the community. "There will be more joy in heaven over the sinner who repents than over 99 righteous persons who need no repentance."

The similarities and the differences in these two versions of the parable of The Lost Sheep have implications for us today. In both Matthew and Luke, the shepherd goes in search of a single missing sheep, and is very glad when he finds it. In

Matthew he searches for the lost sheep because that is his job as a shepherd, reflecting the fact that God does not desire that anyone should be lost. Luke stresses that the lost sheep actually belongs to the one who goes looking. In Matthew, the shepherd's joy is a private affair; this is in keeping with the rest of the chapter, which emphasizes that we should not publicize the fact that a believer has strayed. In Luke, the opposite is the case; it is important to illustrate that those who have been excluded are now included.

So how do we reconcile the differences between the two Gospels? How can we privately seek out one who has gone astray and at the same time restore people to the community from which they have been lost? The first step is to remember that these stories are meant to illustrate principles, not offer strict guidelines.

We can draw two points from Matthew: God does not desire people to be lost; and we must not draw attention to ourselves when we take God's words to heart and seek out those who have "gone astray." Similarly, Luke teaches that since each of us has a responsibility for the lost, we must seek them out. Just as importantly, "the lost" include not only "sinners," but the poor, the sick, the elderly, the homeless, immigrants and all those who wait to participate fully in our faith communities and in society as a whole.

6

The Unmerciful Slave

"Should you not have had mercy
on your fellow slave?"
Matthew 18:23-35

Jesus told this parable in response to a question from Peter, who had asked how often he should forgive someone who had sinned against him. Peter suggested that forgiving someone seven times should be enough, but Jesus went much further, suggesting that we forgive 77 times. Then he told this story about two slaves who each owed different sums of money.

The parable begins with a slave who owed his master, the king, 10,000 talents. This amount does not mean much to most people today; the talent is no longer part of any country's currency, so it is not easy to convert it into dollars. What's more, the talent was the largest denomination used in the Roman Empire, and 10,000 was the largest number used. Therefore, many modern versions of the Bible translate it simply as "a large sum," which weakens the effect of the parable, since one of its points is to contrast the amount that this slave owed his master and the amount that his fellow slave owed him.

The best way to understand the value of a talent is to compare it with the *denarius*, which was the standard daily wage for a labourer. One talent equalled 6000 *denarii*, or about sixteen-and-a-half years' wages (assuming that the person worked seven days a week and took no holidays). It would take the average worker 165,000 years with no time off to earn 10,000 talents, and only if he didn't spend any of his income. When we take into account the interest that would be added to the debt every year, the amount of time required to repay the debt expands even more. Obviously, unless the person had significant resources from somewhere else, he would never be able to pay off such a debt.

The king, realizing that the slave could not pay him back, ordered that the man, his family and his possessions be sold. The sale would not bring in anything close to 10,000 talents, but at least the king could regain some of what he was owed. On hearing of his master's plan, the slave fell to his knees and begged the king to be patient, promising to pay him "everything," although of course this was impossible. Slaves in the ancient world did not even earn a daily wage.

In response to this plea, the king had mercy on the man and forgave the entire debt. What an unexpected and generous action! This should have taught the slave an important lesson about mercy, but when he met up with a fellow slave who owed him 100 *denarii*, not only did he demand immediate payment, but he physically attacked the man, grabbing him by the throat. The second slave replied with the very same words (except one) that the first slave had spoken to their master: "Have patience with me, and I will pay you." The only thing he leaves out is the word "everything." This may reflect Matthew's desire to highlight how great the first slave's debt was, especially compared to the amount he himself was owed; in any case, the second slave does not need to say he will repay "everything," because his debt, equalling 100 days' wages, was manageable. It would take some time for a slave to gather that amount, but it could be done.

The first slave, who moments before had been forgiven an amount 60 million times greater than what he himself was owed, would hear nothing of it. The one who had been shown such great mercy was incapable of showing any mercy at all, and had the slave thrown into prison until the debt was paid. The other slaves were understandably upset. When they complained to their master, the king immediately summoned the unmerciful slave and "handed him over to be tortured until he would pay his entire debt." Once again, we know he can never repay it, but now the slave is in an even worse situation than before: rather than just being sold, he will be tortured until he eventually dies.

In case we miss the point, Jesus adds his own comment on the parable: "So my heavenly Father will also do to every one of you, if you do not

forgive your brother or sister from your heart."
This "moral" has implications for how we
understand the question and answer that
prompted the parable. Peter had asked whether he
should forgive a member of the community who
had sinned against him "as many as seven times."
This number is not random; it reflects the biblical
tradition in which the number seven symbolized
fullness, completion and even perfection. As such,
forgiving someone seven times implies meeting a
lofty standard, and may even hint at the moral
character of the one who forgives: Proverbs 24:16
says, "though [the righteous] fall seven times, they
will rise again." Peter may be implying here that
forgiveness only be given to the righteous: namely,
those who are essentially good but still make
minor slips.

In response, Jesus tells him that he must forgive
not seven times, but 77 times. Why 77? To answer
that question, we need to go back to the story of
Lamech (Genesis 4:23-24). Lamech was a
descendent of Cain, the son of Adam and Eve who
had murdered his brother, Abel. Lamech took
Cain's violence to greater extremes, killing a young
man who had wounded him and boasting that he,
Lamech, would exact 77-fold vengeance upon
anyone who harmed him. Jesus turns this boast
inside out: instead of 77-fold vengeance, he asks
for 77-fold forgiveness. Forgiveness is not only to
be limitless, but is to be offered even to the worst
offenders, including people like Lamech.

More importantly, Jesus' interpretation of the parable reveals that he was not approaching the problem like a mathematical equation. The fact that Peter suggests a number, even the number of perfection, shows that he did not yet understand Jesus' teachings. Christian forgiveness must come "from your heart." As long as we continue to think in terms of how often we are "supposed" to forgive, we run the risk of eventually thinking that we have fulfilled our quota. Worse still, we might keep track of how often we have forgiven certain people so we know when we have reached our limit and can stop. But if we are only willing to forgive a certain number of times, then we never truly forgive at all. True forgiveness, which comes from the heart, means letting go of the offence immediately and completely.

At the same time, we should not forget the amounts of money involved, especially the 10,000 talents owed by the first slave. This amount is important on two levels. First, many of Jesus' listeners would remember that when the Romans occupied their land in 63 BCE, they exacted a tribute of 10,000 talents from the inhabitants. Therefore, for the Jews of Jesus' day, forgiving a debt of the same amount would suggest that God was reversing their occupation and freeing them from the oppression of the Roman Empire. But when the slave uses his own liberation as an opportunity to oppress his fellow servant, he shows that he has failed to understand his master's act of mercy as the way to establish new relationships with others.

Since the king had forgiven a debt that echoed the people's domination by the Romans, the slave should have imitated him by freeing the one who owed him far less.

At the same time, the immensity of the debt is obvious and intentional. Since the king symbolizes God, the 10,000 talents in turn symbolizes the debt that God has forgiven each of us. By using such a large amount, the parable conveys in concrete terms how great are God's mercy and forgiveness towards each of us. When we consider what this parable says about how God treats us, we should respond by treating others – whose debt to us, whether it is monetary or some offence against us, is tiny in comparison – with the same mercy and forgiveness. We are called to act as God acts, and forgive "from the heart."

7

The Good Samaritan

"Who is my neighbour?"
Luke 10:25-37

A lawyer once asked Jesus what he needed to do "to inherit eternal life." Jesus in turn asked him what the Torah (the first five books of the Bible) says on the subject. The man replied, "Love God and love your neighbour." Then he said, "Who is my neighbour?" Jesus responded with a story. A man travelling from Jerusalem to Jericho was attacked by robbers and left "half dead." Both a priest and a Levite passed by, but neither stopped to help. Then a Samaritan came along and, "moved with pity," tended to the injured man's wounds and then took him to an inn and cared for him overnight. The next day he gave the innkeeper two *denarii* (two days' wages) to look after the man, and promised that he would pay any additional expenses when he returned from his journey.

This parable contains a twist that would have been immediately obvious to a first-century Palestinian audience, although it might not be to us. For them, a Samaritan helping a Jew was inconceivable. This animosity went both ways: a Samaritan would have been equally scandalized if one of his people helped a Jew.

To understand this mutual distrust, which was often closer to hatred, we need to go back about 750 years. In 722 BCE, the Assyrians, centred in what is northern Iraq today, conquered the northern kingdom of Israel and incorporated it into their empire. The central section of northern Israel was made into the Assyrian province of Samaria. Moreover, the Assyrians put into practice their main tactic for preventing future rebellions in the provinces, what we might call "limited ethnic cleansing." They would take a portion of the native population from a region and scatter those people throughout their vast empire. They would then take people from a number of different provinces and bring them to the newly conquered region. Cutting both groups of people off from their homelands made them less likely to seek independence. At the same time, those who were left in their native land would barely constitute a majority, and therefore were also less likely to rebel.

Gradually, the Israelites of Samaria intermarried with the diverse peoples who were settled there by the Assyrians. As a result, the Israelites living in the south viewed the Samarians with suspicion. In their opinion, not only were the Samarians no longer "pure" Israelites, but their marriages to other peoples raised the possibility that they had also been contaminated by foreign religions (see 2 Kings 17:24-34; cf. Sirach 50:25-26). For instance, when the people of Samaria offered to help rebuild the temple in Jerusalem after it was destroyed by the Babylonians in 587 BCE their offer was rejected (Ezra 4:1-3). But the Samarians considered themselves true and faithful Israelites, even if their neighbours to the south did not. They had their own version, with only minor variations, of the Torah; they even had their own temple where they worshipped the LORD, since they were not permitted to worship in Jerusalem. Their temple was destroyed by a Jewish army in the late second century BCE, which only served to drive the two groups even further apart.

The result was that by the Second Testament period, the relationship between the Samaritans, as they were then known, and the Jews of both Galilee to their north and Judea to their south, was anything but friendly. They viewed each other with suspicion at the best of times and hostility at the worst of times. The first attitude is reflected in John 4:9, where a Samaritan woman asks Jesus, "How is it that you, a Jew, ask a drink of me, a woman of Samaria?" John follows this with the understated comment that "Jews do not share things in common with Samaritans." The second attitude can be seen in Matthew 10:5, where Jesus tells the disciples not to go into pagan territory or enter a Samaritan town. Luke 9:51-56 shows what could happen when a Jew did enter Samaritan territory: the Samaritans refused the traditional offer of hospitality to strangers, so James and John reacted by seeking to call down lightning on the town, which Jesus forbade. That episode also shows why most Jews travelling from Galilee to Jerusalem took a much longer route that went around Samaritan territory.

So it is clear why a "good" Samaritan would be so shocking to Jesus' contemporaries. This story goes against everything they believed about Samaritans. In fact, the lawyer's initial reference to Scripture probably was meant to exclude such people. When asked what the scriptures said was necessary for eternal life, he referred to Deuteronomy 6:5, which concerns love of God, and Leviticus 19:18, which identifies his "neighbour" as his "people." Indeed, Leviticus 19:18 limits the obligations due to one's neighbour to the Jewish people. And that may very well have been the man's intention: to limit the number of people he had to consider his neighbour, and therefore worthy of his love. But this parable tells us to look beyond such narrow categories in identifying our neighbour. It switches the focus from who is *my* neighbour to who *acts like* a neighbour. According to a strict reading of Leviticus 19:18, a Samaritan would never be a neighbour to a Jew, and yet, "moved with pity," a Samaritan acted like a neighbour anyway.

The Samaritan's actions are compared to those of two leading members of Jewish society at the time: a priest and a Levite. Neither one helped the man who was left "half dead" at the side of the road. According to the Torah, touching a corpse made a person ritually impure, and it took seven days of ritual purification for that impurity to be removed (see Leviticus 21:1-3, 11; Numbers 5:2; 19:11-20 [especially v. 16]; Ezekiel 44:25-27). So if a priest touched a dead person he would not be able to offer sacrifice in the temple for a week and a Levite would be unable to fulfill his role as a temple servant. From the road, it may have been hard to tell if the man was half dead or completely dead, and so the priest and the Levite erred on the side of caution. To give them the benefit of the doubt, perhaps they intended to send someone else back to investigate the matter further. But the Samaritan came upon the scene before any alternative arrangements could be made and took care of the wounded man himself.

At the end of the parable, Jesus turned to the man who had asked him what he needed to do to inherit eternal life and said, "Which of these three, do you think, was a neighbour to the man who fell into the hands of the robbers?" His answer was "The one who showed him mercy." The man's original question – "Who is my neighbour?" – has been well answered by the parable, which shows what it means to act like a neighbour: what helps us determine when to offer our help is whether someone needs it.

The parable of The Good Samaritan, therefore, changes the question from "Who is my neighbour?" to "What does it mean for me to be a neighbour?" The point is not who shares my ethnic identity but rather who needs my help. The man who asked the first question may have sought to avoid the second question, just as he sought "to justify himself." His question was less about who needed his help than about how many people he was *required* to help.

Things have not changed much in the last 2000 years. Many people today are overly concerned with just the minimum they "have to" give to others. The parable of The Good Samaritan challenges us to rethink our attitude.

This parable has significant implications for our modern world. Many people today argue that we should look after "our own" first, and try to define our "neighbour" in very narrow terms, excluding immigrants from certain countries, or people of other faiths or races, for example. But in the parable, the beaten man's true "neighbour" was someone who the man's actual neighbours would have rejected. If we truly learn this parable's lesson, we will treat all we meet as our neighbour.

8

The Rich Fool

"This very night your life
is being demanded of you."
Luke 12:16-21

Jesus' attitude towards money is generally at odds with that of our modern materialistic society. He knew that money could become an end in itself, with people desiring to possess it only for their own benefit, or worse, simply for the sake of having it. The parable of The Rich Fool illustrates what happens when we do not keep money in the proper perspective.

Most of the parable consists of a rich man's internal thoughts about his possessions. After the introductory statement that his property had yielded an abundance of crops, he muses about what to do about this "problem." Since his barns are full, he decides to tear them down and build bigger ones to hold all his possessions. Then he will be able to relax and enjoy what he has for the rest of what he expects to be a very long life. However, that very night God brings his life to an end, and he does not benefit from his goods.

The folly of focusing our lives on acquiring material possessions is a common theme of Israel's wisdom tradition. The book of Qoheleth (Ecclesiastes) comments more than once on someone who stores up goods that he never gets to enjoy, either because he puts it off or because he dies suddenly (cf. Qoh 5:13-14; 6:1-6). Even closer to the parable is Sirach 11:19, which speaks of a rich man who, "when he says, 'I have found rest, and now I shall feast on my goods!' he does not know how long it will be until he leaves them to others and dies." The general situation is so similar to the parable that the text from Sirach may well have inspired the parable.

Another aspect to both texts suggests the similarity is more than accidental. Sirach 11:18 tells us that this person became rich through a miser's life (the NRSV translation, which says that he does so "through diligence and self-denial," is wrong; the Hebrew says he does so "by afflicting himself" and the ancient Greek version translated this as "by clinging and grasping"; cf. Sirach 14:3-10). His acquisition of wealth came through selfishness; he was concerned with how he alone might benefit, with no thought for the good of others. In the same way, the Rich Fool is a self-centred man. In the four short verses in which the man talks to himself he repeats "I" six times and "my" five times. There is not even a passing thought about others, no consideration whether the hungry or poor might benefit from the blessing he has received, no desire to share his money with the less fortunate. It is this selfish attitude, and not just his possession of wealth, that is criticized in the parable.

The term God uses for the man – "fool" – hints at why this is the case. In the First Testament, the fool is the person who rejects the way of life that God has planned for the world as a whole and for Israel in particular. In fact, the Greek term in Luke is exactly the same as the one used in the Greek translation of Psalm 14:1 – "Fools say in their hearts 'There is no God.'" The rich man has not actually said those words, but what he did say was spoken to himself, that is, in his heart. Furthermore, his words reveal that his possessions have become the most important thing in his life. They have even become his God. His failure is not a case of "theoretical" atheism, denying the existence of God on an intellectual level, but a form of "practical" atheism that denies the active power of God in one's life. By thinking that his happiness came from his possessions, he was, in effect, denying that God is the source and preserver of his life.

Lest we miss this point, Luke has surrounded the parable with warnings about the proper use of wealth. Just before the parable, Jesus warned two brothers who were feuding over their inheritance to be wary of greed, pointing out that "one's life does not consist in the abundance of possessions" (v. 15). This view is reinforced by the summary statement found after the parable that the fate of the Rich Fool will be shared by "those who store up treasures for themselves but are not rich toward God." Being "rich toward God" means using our possessions as God desires, for the good of others, not hoarding them for our benefit alone. Finally, immediately following the parable we find sayings about trusting in God for what we need, with Jesus urging the disciples to store up "treasure in heaven" (Luke 12:33; cf. 18:22) rather than amassing wealth on earth.

Things are much the same today. Western society's concern with acquiring things has spread to much of the world. Commerce and economics take precedence over justice and human rights. The primary concern of most companies is for more consumers to buy their goods, regardless of whether they need or can afford those things. What really matters is that companies maintain their profit levels. To that end, manufacturers lay off long-time employees in order to reduce costs so that the shareholders can receive a bigger dividend, with little consideration for the fate of those workers. Society is driven by greed, not compassion.

Yet, just like the Rich Fool, people's obsession with wealth has sometimes led to catastrophe. When the stock market plunges, billions of dollars are lost in a short time. Many of those who put their faith in increasing profits are left with nothing. Nonetheless, as the stock market begins to climb, people again put their life savings into it. Similarly, executives lie about the value of their companies and falsify records in order to lure more money into their coffers. But when the truth is revealed those companies collapse, and the investors are left with little or nothing.

This parable warns us to avoid falling into greed. It does not say that possessions themselves are evil, or argue against investing in a solid retirement plan. But it does subordinate such things to our relationship with God, and thus to our relationships with others. The danger in becoming rich is that we may forget God, others, or even both. That is why Jesus says elsewhere, "It is easier for a camel to go through the eye of a needle than for someone who is rich to enter the kingdom of God" (Luke 18:25). It is not impossible, but great wealth does make it difficult.

9

The Great Dinner/Banquet

"Bring in the poor, the crippled, the blind,
and the lame."
Luke 14:16-24 and Matthew 22:1-10

At first glance, the stories of The Great Dinner in Luke and The Great Banquet in Matthew are different enough that one might think they are two different parables. However, the basic details are the same in both Gospels, which suggests that they are based on a common source, probably the Q document. Luke's story, which is simpler and less allegorical than Matthew's, is probably closer to the original version; Matthew seems to have developed it more in light of the early history of the Church. For this reason, it is best to start with Luke's version and then look at Matthew's additional elements.

In Luke, a man decides to give a great dinner and invites many guests. Little is said about his identity, but we can assume from the scale of the feast that he is a man of some importance and wealth. The initial guests received at least two invitations: the first when he announced the dinner, and the second when he sent his slave to tell them the dinner was ready. But when the second invitation arrived, the guests began to make excuses.

Even though many were invited, only three people's excuses are narrated. This is in keeping with the ancient "rule of three," in which describing something three times stands as a summary for all the times similar things might have occurred. These three individuals stand for all those who had been invited but now find themselves unable or unwilling to attend. Perhaps they have other plans for that time, or no longer want to go. Whatever their reason, the excuses they give are not good ones. One claims he has to inspect some newly purchased land, another has bought some oxen, and a third is newly married. Regardless of the validity of such excuses, in the ancient world their refusal to honour an invitation they had previously accepted would have been a major insult. The fact that the invitation was to share a meal, one of the highest forms of hospitality in that culture, makes the insult even greater.

The slave reports back to his master, who then sends him out into the streets to "bring in the poor, the crippled, the blind, and the lame." This picks up on the previous section of Luke's Gospel, where Jesus had told the guests at a meal that they should not seek the places of honour at the table, in case someone more important than they arrived and they had to vacate their seat (Luke 14:7-10). In the ancient world this was more than just embarrassing; it would have brought shame to the person who had claimed more honour than was deserved. Embarrassment is what we feel when we have done something wrong or out of place, whereas shame results from the attitudes of others about us. The opposite of shame is honour, which also depends on the opinions of others rather than on our own self-image. In the ancient world it was honour and shame that mattered; what people thought of themselves was irrelevant.

Jesus' second piece of advice to his fellow diners was that they should not invite those who could repay the invitation. Once again, his instructions were given against the background of the rules of honour and shame, since one of the ways people were honoured was precisely through such invitations. Instead, Jesus said that they should invite "the poor, the crippled, the lame, and the blind," precisely the groups that the homeowner in the parable of The Great Dinner now invites. After those with fields, livestock and new wives (namely, those who would have been in a position to return the man's hospitality) decline, the homeowner follows Jesus' earlier advice and brings in those who have no means to reciprocate. The man has abandoned the rules of honour and shame: since the dinner is prepared and those for whom it was intended have rejected it, others who would normally never have been invited into "polite" society will get to enjoy it. In fact, when there are not even enough of them to fill the dining hall the homeowner tells his slave to force passersby to come to the meal so that nothing will go to waste.

An allegorical aspect to the story is evident in Luke's version. Christians hearing this parable would associate the meal with the messianic banquet established by Jesus. The delayed invitation could stand either for the First Testament and its subsequent fulfillment in the person of Jesus, or else the initial proclamation of the gospel by Jesus, followed by the activity of Christian missionaries, including the Gospel writers. In either case, if those to whom the message is initially addressed refuse to accept it, then it will be given to others. The messianic feast requires a full dining hall.

Matthew makes the allegorical interpretation of the parable more explicit through a series of changes and additions. In Matthew the dinner is a wedding banquet a king holds for his son. The king sends more than just one slave, and does so three times. This not only enhances the drama of the narrative, but once again uses the rule of three to indicate that the king has made every reasonable effort to have the guests come. Once the banquet is ready, those who were invited earlier simply refuse to come. After the second invitation, one individual goes to his farm and another to his business, while the rest "seized [the king's] slaves, mistreated them, and killed them." In response, the king orders his troops to burn their city, then sends his slaves out to bring in "both good and bad."

The Christian reading of this story is straightforward: the king is God, his son is Jesus and the wedding banquet is a common image for the early Eucharist. The death of the slaves alludes to the First Testament prophets who were often called God's servants (e.g., 2 Kings 9:7; Ezra 9:11; Jeremiah 7:25; Ezekiel 38:17; Daniel 9:6; Amos 3:7; Zechariah 1:6; the Greek word *doulos* can mean either slave or servant). Note, too, that later in Matthew Jesus calls Jerusalem "the city that kills the prophets" (Matthew 23:37). Matthew's Christian allegory also reflects the fate of Jerusalem, which was burned by the Roman legions in 70 CE, just as the city in the parable was burned by the king's troops. Finally, the mixed nature of the eventual guests at the banquet, both good and bad, recognizes that the early Church was an imperfect institution made up of diverse people (cf. the parable of The Wheat and the Weeds, found only in Matthew 13:24-30; see Chapter 3 in this book).

So far Matthew has been expanding upon aspects of the story that are also found in Luke, but he adds another episode at the end. Once the "good and bad" have been assembled, the king enters and sees a man who is not wearing a "wedding robe." One could object that if he was just brought in from the streets, then of course he would not have such a garment, but that would miss the point. The king's inspection of the guests refers to the Last Judgment, by which time people were expected to have prepared themselves. This additional material is Matthew's way of dealing with the mixed nature of the early Christian community. It was composed of both "good and bad," but that was not to be taken as a licence for the "bad" to remain bad. They were indeed allowed into the wedding banquet, which symbolized the community's eucharistic meal, but that was to be a means of preparing themselves for the coming judgment. By then, even those who were not properly attired when they first entered the banquet should have made themselves so, and those who refuse to do so will be excluded.

God's desire to enter into a deeper relationship with us, symbolized in the ancient world through the intimacy of sharing a meal, continues today. This invitation is extended through the Scriptures, through the ministry of the churches, through homilies, and through the direct call of the Holy Spirit. But just like the guests in the parable, we have the freedom to accept or reject the invitation. In fact, even if we do initially accept it, we are still free to refuse God's love at a later point.

At the same time, God extends the invitation to all. God does not just invite the righteous, or the morally good, or the spiritual people among us. God also invites those we would not think to invite. Luke describes them as "the poor, the crippled, the blind, and the lame." These were the people who were considered unimportant in ancient society. In fact, those unenviable conditions were often seen as an indication of sin, as a punishment from God. As a result, such people were generally excluded, and forced to live on the margins of the community. In some cases this even meant having to live outside the city itself, but it almost always meant being left out of the daily life of the city.

We would do well to ask ourselves who in our modern society is marginalized. If we are going to be God's true servants, the messengers of the gospel, then it is our job to identify those who are excluded, to seek them out and invite them to join our faith communities, and then to welcome them. If along the way we wind up with both the good and bad, even in a moral sense, so be it. If we do our best to live the gospel message, people will be inspired to change for the better. God does not require us to be perfect before inviting us in; God only asks that we make the effort to change once we have been admitted.

10

The Prodigal and His Brother

"He was lost and has been found."
Luke 15:11-32

The parable of The Prodigal Son is found only in Luke, and appears immediately after the parables of The Lost Sheep (see Chapter 5 of this book) and The Lost Coin. It makes the same point as those two parables – that God longs for the return of those who have moved away from him – but expressing this idea in terms of a son who leaves his father makes this parable more poignant and effective. Because the drama of the story and the actions of the characters are so engaging, this is one of the more famous of all the parables recorded in the Gospels.

The story begins with a man and his two sons. The younger son asks for his inheritance immediately, rather than waiting until he would normally receive it, which was when his father died. This amounts to wishing his father was dead. It is difficult to imagine a more ungrateful or selfish son, and the reaction of many fathers would be to disown him. Instead, this father complies with his request and gives his younger son the share of his property that would eventually come to him.

Once he has this inheritance, the son further insults his father by taking what he has been given and moving away. He doesn't just move out of the house or to a nearby town – he packs up his property and travels to a "distant country." Once he has what he wants, he abandons his father. This was a direct violation of the Fourth Commandment: "Honour your father and your mother." (Exodus 20:12; Deuteronomy 5:16)This commandment was not just about little children being obedient. It was addressed to adults, and dealt with the obligation of adult children to care for their aged parents who could no longer work or support themselves. Through his actions the younger son displayed total disrespect, not only for his own flesh and blood but also for the divinely revealed religious traditions of his people.

When he gets to the other country, the young man quickly wastes his inheritance, and when famine strikes, he is reduced to working in a pig sty. The irony here is that the one who flaunted one of the Jewish laws, the Fourth Commandment, now finds himself surrounded by swine, which according to Jewish law were unclean animals. Even worse, he begins to hunger for some of the scraps that he is feeding to the pigs. The youth who started out with such arrogance towards his father and his beliefs has fallen low indeed!

Eventually he realizes how much better off he had been at his father's house. Even his father's labourers were treated better than this. So he decides to return home and throw himself on the mercy of his father. To his credit, he knows that his actions towards his father mean that he no longer deserved to be considered the man's son, but he hopes that he can convince his father to hire him like he would any other labourer. At least that would be a step up from his current situation. And so he resolves to return and confess to his father, "I have sinned against heaven and before you." On this point he is correct: not only did his actions break the Fourth Commandment, they also brought shame upon his father (see Chapter 9 of this book for more on the concept of shame in the ancient world).

And so the man heads for home. At this point we encounter the first of two twists in the parable. His father sees him from a distance and, moved by compassion, immediately runs to his son to embrace him. Two points should be noted here. First, the word translated as "compassion" is almost exclusively used in the Second Testament in reference to the compassion of God that is revealed in and through Jesus. Second, the father's actions go against the customs of his culture. The father is a man of substance, one who owns so much property that he requires both slaves and hired labourers to look after it. In that culture such people simply did not run, since that would be an affront to their dignity. Not only that, as a wealthy man he was probably well dressed in a long robe; for him to run he would have to pull up his garment. A wealthy man running down the road with his luxurious robe pulled up around his thighs would be a scandalous sight in the eyes of those who happened to be watching.

Even worse, he runs to meet the very son who had abandoned him, which would have shamed the father further in his neighbours' eyes. Many people in the same situation would have turned away or gone inside the house in order to force the offending son to come to them. At the very least, they would have waited for such an ungrateful son to approach and ask for forgiveness. But not this father. He acts in a way that not only reminds everyone of the shame this son has caused him; he shames himself even more by racing to meet him.

And it doesn't stop there! The son begins his carefully rehearsed speech, asking forgiveness and seeking employment, but before he can get to the second part his father cuts him off. He orders the slaves to bring a robe – not just any robe, but "the best one" – so that his son may be dressed in an honourable fashion. He tells them to put a ring on his finger as a sign of authority, and to put shoes on him to symbolize their acceptance of his authority. Last but not least, to celebrate his son's return he orders them to kill a fatted calf, one that has been fed for some time in preparation for a special occasion.

No wonder this is sometimes called the parable of The Prodigal *Father*. The father does everything a respectable person would *not* do in this situation. He opens himself up to ridicule from his neighbours, and even risks having his son take his forgiveness for granted. Some might think that the father should have laid down some ground rules if the son was going to re-enter the household. But the father does not care about that. What does matter to him is that "this son of mine was dead and is alive again; he was lost and is found!"

But that is not the end of the story. In a second twist, the older brother, the one who had remained faithful to his father after his younger brother's disrespect, comes in from the field and hears the noise of the celebration. When he is told that his father is throwing a party because his brother has returned, he refuses to go in. Instead, he stays outside and sulks. He acts like many people would: it is bad enough that his father is taking back his wild, self-centred brother, but killing the fatted calf for him is going too far.

Now the father risks losing his other son, but for the opposite reason. The younger son did not observe the rules of his society; the elder one observes them too strictly. So, acting in a most undignified manner once again, the father goes outside to his older son and reminds him of his love for him, assuring him that he will still receive his inheritance. He insists that the return of his wayward son is such a wonderful event that they have to celebrate and rejoice.

It is clear that the father in this parable represents God. Apart from the fact that his actions are more extravagant than those of most human beings, we noted earlier that the Greek word used for the father's compassion is used of God most other times in the Gospels. Just as the parables of The Lost Sheep (Luke 15:1-7) and The Lost Coin (Luke 15:8-10) communicate God's desire that sinners return and emphasize the heavenly joy when they do, the parable of The Prodigal Son makes the same points in even more striking terms. It is a great comfort to know that no matter how much we have sinned, God is always willing to take us back if we return to God. The joy that the father in the parable feels when he throws a banquet for his repentant son is but a taste of God's joy when we repent.

But we should not forget the older brother. Would our reaction be any different from his? Those who live a life of fidelity to God, always following the commandments and never committing any grave sin, might easily fall into the trap of the older brother, requiring greater signs of contrition than the father does. Shouldn't "sinners" be reminded of their sin, and of the great mercy that has been shown to them? Not so, according to the prodigal father. We are simply to rejoice that they have returned. All is forgiven!

We can extend this attitude beyond the realm of moral or religious "sin" to include, for example, those who have transgressed against our society, whether by flaunting its conventions or by committing a crime. Are we prepared to welcome them back, no matter how serious their actions against us? Are we able to celebrate their return? It is clear what the father in the parable would do. Can we open our hearts and do the same?

11

The Dishonest Manager

"The children of this age are more shrewd
in dealing with their own generation
than are the children of light."
Luke 16:1-8

This is a difficult parable to understand. The hero of the parable is a dishonest man who cheats his employer and then, when his dishonesty is discovered, cheats even more. How can such an individual be a model for us? The answer may seem as confusing as the parable itself: we are supposed to be like him without being like him.

Jesus tells the story of a rich man's manager. It was this manager's job to look after the rich man's affairs, and especially to organize his business dealings. As the parable moves forward we learn that one of his responsibilities was to take care of his employer's debts. He had the authority to make loans, set the terms and collect the payments in his employer's name. Whenever the manager entered into a transaction, it was understood that he was acting for the rich man, and therefore that his actions had his employer's support and financial backing.

At some point the rich man learns that his manager has been "squandering his property" and demands an immediate accounting of his activities, after which he will fire the manager. We are not told the exact nature of this offence, whether he was mismanaging or embezzling, but in light of his subsequent actions the latter is the more likely case. Moreover, the manager appears to be guilty, since he makes no attempt to defend himself. Instead, he prepares for his life without this job. He does not want to do physical labour and is too proud to beg, so he decides to use his former position to win friends among his master's debtors.

To that end, he calls in everyone who owed his master something and reviews their accounts with them. We are not told about each of them, just two representative examples. The first owed 100 jugs of oil. This "jug" was an Israelite measure called a *bath*, which equalled almost 40 litres (10 gallons); 100 baths would be about 4,000 litres (1,000 gallons). The second owed 100 "containers" of wheat (this is the Hebrew word *kor*, which contained 393 litres); thus, his debt is 3,930 litres (about 1,100 bushels) of wheat. These were not small amounts, by any means, which makes what the manager does next all the more significant.

The manager tells the borrowers to rewrite the loan agreements for a lesser amount. Since they had written the original contracts, if they rewrote them and destroyed the original, the replacement copies would be legally valid. He cuts the first debt in half and reduces the second by 20 per cent. He undoubtedly made comparable arrangements with the other debtors as he met with them "one by one." With such large amounts involved, this would have resulted in substantial savings for each person who had borrowed.

Whether the manager is doing this under his employer's orders or out of his own generosity makes little difference to the debtors. The result is the same: each of their debts is reduced. This in turn would have led to much gratitude and goodwill being extended to the manager. He could expect to receive similar generosity from them in the future.

The debtors follow the manager's instructions, not because they are dishonest, but because they do not know that the manager has been dismissed from his position. That is why he tells the first man to "sit down quickly"; he needs to make these arrangements before the word of his disgrace spreads and people realize that he no longer has the authority to do what he is doing. The individual debtors enter into the revised agreements in good faith.

This makes it difficult, if not impossible, for the rich man to reverse the manager's dishonesty. In the first place, it would mean publicly calling attention to the fact that the man who had cheated him once had done so again. In that culture of honour and shame, to be shown up twice by a subordinate would have been unbearable. Moreover, if he did nothing, his debtors would publicly honour him, praising him in the streets for his generosity. However, if he reinstated the original amounts, then he would be dishonoured for refusing to uphold what all thought was a legitimate agreement. And so, he simply commends the manager for acting "shrewdly."

It is important to recognize that Jesus does not commend the dishonest manager, the employer does. By telling the parable, Jesus is not suggesting that we should act dishonestly, manipulating situations for our own benefit and cheating others along the way. Jesus' message in this parable is found in the second half of verse 8, where he says, "The children of this age are more shrewd in dealing with their own generation than are the children of light." He acknowledges the manager's commitment to looking out for himself, his prompt action and cleverness, but this is not the same as approving of his methods.

This parable is a challenge to Christians, both then and now, to be wiser and more resourceful in pursuing their ultimate goal: a mature relationship with God and others. That goal rules out the manager's dishonesty, but we can and should emulate his dedication to achieving the result he desires, especially since our goal is far more important than his. Because our goal is so important, we are to dedicate all our abilities, resources, skill and wisdom to live united to God in love and faith. In turn, such union with God will lead us to work to build God's kingdom in a spirit of love for those around us, thereby creating a community in which God rules.

Neither the manager nor his actions are meant to be models for us. Instead, we are to imitate his commitment to maintaining his lifestyle. We are called to be equally dedicated to establishing the kingdom of God here on earth, without sharing his approach. In short, we are to be like the dishonest manager when it comes to his attitude, but not his methods.

12

The Widow and
the Unjust Judge

"Will he delay long in helping them?"
Luke 18:1-8

In ancient Israel, widows had special
significance. Widows, along with orphans and
foreigners, were singled out in the First Testament.
Why? In the patriarchal society of the biblical
period, having a male relative to look after you,
and especially to protect your legal rights, made a
big difference in your life. Orphans did not have a
father to fill this role. Widows didn't have a male
protector either; they had left their father's house
to marry, and their husband's death left them
vulnerable. Foreigners, not being native Israelites,
had no Israelite relatives, male or otherwise, to
protect them. To compensate for this absence of a
natural protector, the Israelite covenant included
frequent commands to protect these groups. Those
who had no one in particular to look out for their
safety and well-being were to be looked after by
everyone.

These commands for society to care for the orphan, the widow and the stranger are usually followed by a reminder that the Israelites had once been strangers in Egypt, "that house of slavery" (see, for example, Deuteronomy 25:17-18), where they had no legal protection and were enslaved by Pharaoh. They are instructed always to remember their previous state, from which God had liberated them through the Exodus, and make sure not to oppress others, through physical force or legal corruption. Just as the Lord had entered into a covenant with them after freeing them from Egypt, so too they were required to enter into a covenant with one another, and especially with the weakest among them, to keep them from becoming enslaved.

Luke's Gospel reflects those covenantal obligations towards widows. They received special attention from Jesus, and offences against them are roundly condemned (see, for example, Luke 7:11-17 and 20:45–21:4). So when we meet the widow in this parable, we expect her request for legal justice to be met promptly. She fits the definition of a widow: the fact that she herself appears in court, and not a male who makes a petition on her behalf, indicates that she is completely alone. Unfortunately, she is faced with an "unjust" judge who initially refuses even to hear her case. By doing so, this judge was violating the covenant established by God and supported by Jesus. The emphasis on her pleas for justice and the judge's unjust character calls to mind certain prophetic texts denouncing judges who refused to consider a widow's lawsuit justly (e.g., Jeremiah 5:28 and Zechariah 7:9-10). Through their injustice the judges were not just mistreating fellow Israelites, they were exploiting the powerless in society.

None of that matters to the judge in the parable who, in his own words, had "no fear of God and no respect for anyone." Neither the possibility of divine intervention now, nor punishment after death, nor consideration for the widow's weak position within society, has any effect on his point of view. However, the woman persists (we don't know for how long), and the judge finally gives in to her pleading and delivers a just verdict, in order to be rid of her.

Jesus contrasts this judge with God. If even this unjust judge eventually responds to the widow's persistent pleading and helps her, we can be sure that the God of justice and love will answer us quickly when we pray!

Jesus introduces this parable as being about the "need to pray always and not to lose heart," but that is not really what it teaches. The point is not that if we pray long enough and hard enough we can wear God down. God is not like the unjust judge, who had to be pestered at length before he would render the justice expected of him. God does the opposite, and is always willing to give us what we truly need (although probably not everything we want). God is by nature just, so if what we need is justice, God will be sure to grant it.

Since the parable isn't really about the "need to pray always and not to lose heart," we need to look for some other interpretation. A clue may be found in Jesus' question at the very end of the passage: "When the Son of Man comes, will he find faith on earth?" The early Christians expected Jesus to return soon, within their lifetime, as the glorified Son of Man. It is clear from his writings that Paul, for example, expected to live long enough to witness Jesus coming down from heaven seated upon the clouds (e.g., 1 Thessalonians 4:15, 17).

But almost 2,000 years have passed since then and Jesus has yet to appear in that way. How can we maintain our faith in him in light of such a great delay? One way is consistent daily prayer. Regular prayer should focus on entering into an ongoing relationship with God, rather than on asking God for things. Just as we need to nurture our human relationships with family and friends, we also need to nurture our relationship with God. When people stop communicating they tend to drift apart, which makes it even harder to communicate. As a result, the relationship often breaks down completely, such that people become strangers to one another and go their separate ways.

Healthy daily prayer should focus on talking to God and listening for a response. Although there will be times when we ask things of God, our goal should be to move towards a pattern of mutual communication. Regular prayer helps us maintain an ongoing relationship with God, which in turn establishes a pattern of answered prayer, prayer where we are attuned to God's response. When that happens, we will know that God answers prayer by entering into a relationship of love and concern with us. Unlike the unjust judge, who only responds after repeated requests, God's very nature is to desire a relationship with us, and so God answers quickly and frequently.

Seen in this light, the parable of the persistent widow is not about repeated prayer for one particular short-term thing, but faithfulness to prayer itself. That God will be faithful in answering our prayer goes without saying. The real question is whether we, through the practice of ongoing prayer, will be faithful to God.

13

The Pharisee
and the Tax Collector

"This man went down to his home justified."
Luke 18:9-14

In order to understand this parable fully, we
need to look closely at the two characters: the
Pharisee and the tax collector. Many people today
have a negative view of Pharisees, especially in
terms of their character, based partly on a superficial
reading of texts like this one. They may not realize
why a Pharisee would have had such a negative
opinion of a tax collector. Why would someone who
collected taxes be the brunt of such scorn? Once
these issues have been clarified, we will have a solid
background for interpreting the parable.

Although the Pharisees did not make up a large
portion of the population of Israel, they were an
important group in Judaism at the time of Jesus,
and were even more important during the early
history of the Church. After Jerusalem was
destroyed by the Romans, most other Jewish
groups were either eliminated or became

insignificant. Only the Pharisees and the Jewish-Christians had any real importance in terms of the religious life of the people. In fact, by the time the Gospels were written, these two groups were competing with each other over what it meant to be a Jew. Thus, many of the Gospel stories about the Pharisees reflect their opposition to the early Jewish Church over the correct interpretation of Jewish traditions, and especially over whether believing in Jesus was compatible with Judaism. The Jewish-Christians, of course, did not see any conflict between Judaism and their belief that Jesus was the Messiah, but the Pharisees disagreed. For the most part, the Gospels reflect the opposition between the two groups at the time the Gospels were written rather than at the time Jesus lived.

We should be clear, however, that the Pharisees were not a group of legalists, characterized by hypocrisy. They began as a renewal movement within Judaism that promoted devotion and piety. Their aim was to make sure that people observed the Torah (the first five books of the Bible) properly, since it was the basis of the covenant, which established a special relationship between God and the people of Israel. The requirements of the Torah set Israel apart from other nations and recognized them as God's chosen people. So although people did not always agree with the Pharisees' strict interpretation of some elements of the Torah, most Jews hearing this story would have had a neutral or slightly positive reaction to the term "Pharisee."

"Tax collector," on the other hand, would have provoked the opposite response. In the Roman Empire, tax collectors were not civil servants who earned a set salary like their modern counterparts do. People got their position as tax collector by agreeing to gather a certain amount of money; whoever promised the most got the job. It wasn't enough to collect this quota for the Romans; a tax collector only earned enough money to live on by gathering more than he promised to turn in and keeping the difference. Taxes were not determined in proportion to one's earnings, or a set percentage added to one's purchases in the form of sales tax, but by how much the tax collector could get from each person. The more he could get from people, the greater his profit would be, and threats and even physical violence were often used to increase his profit margin. And if that wasn't bad enough, the taxes themselves went to the Romans. This meant that the Jewish people paid taxes, not to improve their own situation, but to finance the Roman occupation of their land. For this reason, most Jews reviled tax collectors as collaborators with a despised occupying army; some Jews even hated them.

In that context, Jesus' audience would side with a Pharisee over a tax collector every time. In this parable, however, the Pharisee provides a convenient way for Luke to make the point that when we come before God in prayer, we are to do so with humility, not pride. It is precisely because most people would identify this Pharisee as a pious man that his pride and arrogance are so appalling. His attitude contradicts his actions. Note that Luke does not raise any direct objection to the Pharisee's actions in and of themselves. Fasting and tithing were and are commendable, and the Pharisee went beyond the minimum requirements. For instance, the First Testament required fasting only on the Day of Atonement, the holiest day of the Jewish year (Leviticus 16:29-34; 23:27-32; Numbers 29:7). By the first century CE, however, various groups, such as the Essenes, who wrote the Dead Sea Scrolls, practised regular fasting as an act of piety and devotion. The Pharisee in this parable also seems to regard his fasting as a positive thing worth noting; the fact that he specifies doing so twice a week suggests that he goes beyond the normal practice of others.

The Pharisee didn't begrudge God the expected tithe, either. Giving 10 per cent to God is also mandated by the Scriptures, although the requirements differ from one text to another (compare Leviticus 27:30-33 and Numbers 18:20-32 with Deuteronomy 14:22-27; 26:2-13). To be sure he did not cheat God, the Pharisee applied the tithe to "all my income." At first glance this seems to indicate that, in modern terms, he calculated the 10 per cent donation on his gross earnings, not his take-home pay. But the phrase really means "all that I acquire." He is not referring only to what he earns, but also to whatever he buys. Just in case the seller had not offered the tithe on such goods, the Pharisee does so himself.

So the Pharisee did not need to change his basic way of life; his pious acts were worthy of imitation. But his detailed description of them gives us a clue about what is at issue here. He begins by giving thanks to God, but rather than giving thanks for what God has done, he gives thanks for what he himself has done. Instead of making his prayer about God, as he should have, the Pharisee makes it all about himself. What is worse, he thinks his piety proves he is better than others, something he also attributes, not to God, but to his own actions.

In reality, the Pharisee's problem is not his actions but his attitude. He "regarded others with contempt," and so he lists various types of people he considers to be far beneath him. The last and worst of them all is a tax collector who had also come to the temple to pray. Because many Jews despised tax collectors, the fact that he would even approach the temple would have been seen as scandalous.

And yet, the tax collector offers a contrast to the Pharisee in two ways. The first is his physical demeanour. The Pharisee would have entered the main part of the temple and, as was the Jewish custom, found a place where he could stand and raise his hands and eyes to heaven to address God (see Psalm 123:1; John 11:41; 1 Timothy 2:8). The tax collector, on the other hand, stood "far off." He was probably in the temple's outer courtyard, recognizing that he was not worthy to enter such a holy place or be with "holy" people. He does not even dare raise his eyes, lest God think he considered himself able to approach God; instead, he beats his breast as a sign of his anguish and penitence.

The second way the tax collector differs from the Pharisee is the content of his prayer. For one thing, it is much shorter. In English translations of the Bible, the Pharisee spends two verses (33 words) praising himself, whereas the tax collector's words amount to about one quarter of a verse (7 words). Note, too, the content of the prayer, in which the tax collector acknowledges his sinfulness and asks for God's mercy. Where the Pharisee considered prayer an opportunity to remind God how wonderful he himself was, the tax collector saw an opportunity to acknowledge God as the source of mercy and forgiveness.

At the end of the parable, the tax collector is held up as a model for others because he approached God with an honest awareness of his situation and simply pleaded for mercy. Thus the Pharisee is right: he is not like the tax collector, but not quite the way he imagines. He thinks he is better than such a sinful individual, but that very thought negates any spiritual benefit his otherwise positive actions could have brought him.

In contrast, by acknowledging his sinfulness the tax collector is forgiven. Since what matters in prayer is the attitude of the heart, Jesus announces that the tax collector is the one whose prayer was heard and who was justified by God. In the Bible, to be justified means to stand in a right relationship with God. In the First Testament this relationship was expressed in terms of the covenant, the terms of which are spelled out in the Scriptures. But this covenant, by its very nature, links our relationship with God to our relationship with others. One irony of the parable is that the Pharisee, a member of a group that went out of its way to preserve the covenant with God, had actually broken it. By cutting himself off from those he thought beneath him, he also cut himself off from God.

The parable of The Pharisee and the Tax Collector urges us to develop humility, both before God and in relationship to others. Humility is poorly understood these days. Many people confuse it with a negative self-image and a denial of the positive aspects of their lives or the good they do. But being humble does not mean thinking we are worthless, it simply means keeping our worth in its proper perspective. This means always acknowledging the ultimate source of the good we do, and maintaining the proper attitude with respect to that source: God. Only when we start to think that we are ultimately responsible for the positive things in our lives, or that they make us better than anyone else, do we run into danger.

So what are we, Pharisees or tax collectors? Maybe we should be both, combining the actions of the first with the attitude of the second.

14

The Labourers in the Vineyard

"Am I not allowed to do what I choose
with what belongs to me?"
Matthew 20:1-16

In this parable Jesus compares God's reign to a
vineyard, where the landowner is hiring labourers
for the day. A vineyard is a common metaphor for
Israel in the First Testament. The most famous text
to use this imagery is Isaiah 5:1-7, which is itself a
parable; other texts are also found in the prophets
(e.g., Isaiah 27:2-6 and Jeremiah 12:10). Building
upon these references in the First Testament, a
number of texts in the Second Testament also use
the vineyard as a metaphor for God's rule. These
include the parable of The Two Sons (Matthew
21:28-32) and the parable of The Tenants (Mark
12:1-9; see Chapter 15 of this book).

The parable of The Labourers in the Vineyard
relies upon common employment practices in the
Near East, both then and now. Those looking for
work would gather at a particular spot known to
both labourers and employers, and those who
needed workers – for their fields, to load crops for

delivery, or to do unskilled work of any kind – would come and hire as many people as they needed for that day. Such workers were in a vulnerable position. Unlike those with regular jobs, they were dependent on whatever employment they could get from day to day. If they did not find work, they would earn nothing, and they and their families would be unable to buy food or perhaps even secure a place to sleep that night.

In one sense, such day-labourers were in an even worse situation than slaves who, although not free, did not have to worry about such basic necessities of life, since their masters would provide them. As a result, day-labourers could easily be exploited. If a large number of men was looking for work, and few people looking for workers, the employers could force them to work for less than the standard wage, since the alternative might be not to work at all that day.

This is the background against which a landowner went to hire labourers "early in the morning" for his vineyard. The precise time is not given, but since he returns to hire more at nine o'clock, noon and three o'clock, we can assume that this first round of hiring probably occurred at six in the morning. This was, in fact, the normal starting time of the workday, which lasted 12 hours.

The landowner agrees to pay the men hired at six o'clock one *denarius*, which was the standard daily wage. He appears to be a fair man; he is not trying to underpay them. As the story progresses, however, it turns out that he probably could have bargained with them if he had been so inclined, because at nine o'clock he discovers men still waiting in the marketplace to be hired. On this particular day there are more workers available than there are jobs to go around. At that point a shrewd employer could negotiate for even less than three-quarters of a day's wage, but the landowner simply tells them to go work in his vineyard and promises to pay them "whatever is right." This suggests that he will pay them for the portion of the day that they work. Here we may catch a glimpse of the man's character, since it is not clear whether he even needed more workers. Verse 3 merely states that he "went out," without specifying that it was to find more labourers.

The same thing happens again at noon and at three o'clock. Each time he goes out, he finds more men in the marketplace waiting to work, and he "did the same." This should be understood to mean that he not only hires each group, he also promises to pay them "whatever is right," as he did with those hired at nine o'clock. Finally, at five o'clock he finds still more men who had wanted to work that day but were unable to find anyone to hire them. With only one hour left in the workday, he hires them as well and sends them off to his vineyard.

When it comes time to pay the workers, he orders his manager to pay the men in the reverse order of when they were hired. The only reason for doing this was so those who have been working all day can see how much those who worked only one hour are paid. So when those who had worked only one hour rather than the normal 12 hours stepped forward, they probably expected to receive one-twelfth of a *denarius*. Instead, they were given a full day's wage! As a result, those who had worked for the full 12 hours expected to be paid more. That was only "right": they had worked more and so they deserved more. But they, too, received one *denarius*.

Those hired first began to complain loudly to the landowner at being treated exactly the same as the latecomers. Many of us would sympathize with them. They weren't being treated fairly. They had not only worked longer than the others, they had endured the scorching heat of the Middle Eastern midday sun. Yet here they were, being paid no more than those who had worked only the last hour, when most of the work was already done and it was much cooler.

The owner's response to this complaint is instructive. He starts by saying "I am doing you no wrong." Those who were hired first were promised one *denarius* for the day's work, and that is what they receive. He was not cheating them or refusing to honour their initial agreement. The fact that he pays the others the same amount for less work is not injustice to the first group but generosity to the latecomers. And since it is his money, he is free to do as he wishes with it.

There are two different understandings of what is "right" present in the parable. For the workers, what is "right" is that all are paid what they have "earned." If one person works longer or harder than another, then he has "earned" more pay than the other. Even though they initially agreed on the usual day's wage, if the owner decided that the latecomers had "earned" a full day's wage, then since the first group had worked longer, they obviously had "earned" more.

The owner, however, has a different view of what is "right." To begin with, he honoured his original agreement with the first group of workers. He paid them what he promised. He had acknowledged at the beginning of the day that one *denarius* would allow a man to provide for his family. On this basis he then chose to pay every worker the same amount. Rather than determining what is right by calculating what each person has "earned," he considered what each person needs. That is because, as we saw at the beginning of this chapter, the vineyard symbolizes Israel, and its owner is God. God's ways are not our ways (Isaiah 55:8-9). God does not treat us according to what we deserve or what we have earned. If that were the case, then we would be in serious trouble, for none of us deserves God's love and mercy. Instead, God gives us grace, which by definition is something given freely out of love, not because we have earned it.

This brings us back to the earlier suggestion that perhaps the owner may not have needed more workers when he "went out" the second, third and fourth time. If so, he hired them in order to bestow his generosity on them by paying a full day's wage for less than a full day's work. He did not consider what they would "earn" by starting late, nor did he even take into account whether he needed their efforts. His only concern was whether they needed to earn some money. As such, he is an accurate reflection of God, who is always ready to welcome those who need God, no matter when the need is perceived. In fact, just as the landowner kept going out to see if there were still others who could benefit from his generosity, God continually seeks out those who have not yet turned to God and invites them into the vineyard.

But what about us, especially those of us who have been working for God since the beginning of the day? Just as initially we may sympathize with the first group of workers in the parable, so too, we may be tempted to be less than welcoming to those who enter into the community of faith after us. This parable reminds us that we who have known God's grace for some time must not envy those who receive the same measure at a later time. Instead, we are asked to recognize that God welcoming us into the vineyard is also an act of generosity. As the landowner says, "Am I not allowed to do what I choose with what belongs to me?"

At the same time, we must not restrict the parable's significance to the spiritual realm, since people living at the time of Jesus would not have isolated the spiritual aspect of their existence from everyday life. Our modern tendency to separate the two would have been inconceivable to them. The parable can also influence how we view the economic realities of our modern society: if God thinks people should be paid according to what they need in order to provide a decent life for themselves and their families, then we must rethink how things are done today. This might include lobbying to raise the minimum wage, questioning excessive compensation for executives, being more flexible about who is allowed to work and in what jobs, and showing respect to those who earn less or who have less desirable jobs.

The parable also has implications for how we treat those who have not been able to find work at the eleventh hour: the poor, the unemployed, those on welfare, the homeless. Our modern economy does not even come close to embracing what this parable envisions. How can we begin to live the lessons found in the parable in our daily lives and in society as a whole?

15

The Tenants

"What then will the owner
of the vineyard do?"
Mark 12:1-9

This parable is an allegory reflecting on Jesus' entire ministry from a perspective after his death, which is the central part of the parable. The story tells of a landowner who leases his vineyard; the tenants then not only refuse to provide him with the produce they had promised as rent, they beat and even kill the slaves he sends to collect what they owe him. Eventually, he sends his son, whom he assumes they will respect because the son represents the father's authority. But they also kill the son and "threw him out of the vineyard." In response, the vineyard's owner decides to expel the tenants and give the vineyard to others.

As we saw in the previous chapter, in the biblical tradition the vineyard is a symbol for Israel. In fact, this parable draws heavily upon a passage in Isaiah in which the prophet sings a song about his friend's vineyard (Isaiah 5:1-7). Isaiah describes how his friend built a hedge wall around the land, tilled the land, cleared it of stones, planted choice vines, built a watchtower and prepared a wine press, all in anticipation of the grapes that would eventually come. But all the vineyard ever produced was "wild grapes," so the man eventually abandoned it to be trampled and overgrown. The prophet concludes by explicitly identifying the vineyard with Israel, stating that its crime was bloodshed and violence rather than the harvest of justice that God desires.

The vineyard imagery continues elsewhere, in both the First and Second Testaments. Another passage in Isaiah states that God will always protect his "pleasant vineyard," which is once again directly identified as Israel (Isaiah 27:2-6). Similarly, Jeremiah 12:10 complains that the shepherds (i.e., the leaders) have destroyed God's vineyard, his "pleasant portion." In the Second Testament, a vineyard is also a popular image for Israel. In the parable of The Two Sons (Matthew 21:28-32), their father asked them to work in his vineyard, but only one obeyed; the parable of The Workers in the Vineyard (Matthew 20:1-16; see Chapter 14 in this book) also uses the vineyard metaphor. Similarly, Luke 13:6 describes a man who plants a fig tree in his vineyard, but the tree does not bear fruit.

But of all the Second Testament texts that use the metaphor of the vineyard to represent Israel, the parable of The Tenants is the closest to those from the First Testament. Much of the language used to describe the man's preparation of the vineyard in Mark is similar to Isaiah 5:1-2, and at times is identical. Just as the friend in Isaiah did, the man in the parable "planted" a vineyard, built a "fence" around it, dug a "wine press" and "built a watchtower." Even the format of the two parables is the same. The storyteller describes an individual preparing a vineyard and notes that his expectations for it were not met: it yields wild grapes in Isaiah, and in Mark the tenants refuse to pay their rent. After this, the narrator asks what the vineyard owner should do and then provides his own answer, which involves some form of punishment. But there is a difference as well. In Isaiah the problem is with the vineyard, while in Mark the tenants to whom the vineyard has been entrusted are the problem.

The language from Isaiah is not only used because it is part of a familiar parable. It also helps to establish the care the man gave to setting up his vineyard, indicating his devotion to it (Israel) and implying his expectation that the tenants will display similar concern for the vineyard. The fence keeps out those who might trample the vines or eat the grapes, and the watchtower provides a place from which to spot any intruders who get over the wall. Digging a wine press indicates that the man expects the vineyard to yield grapes that would be good enough to be made into wine. And of course he plans to share in the produce. He does not give the field to the tenants, but rather leases it to them.

The standard practice was that tenants would work the field for the owner and pay rent with a portion of the harvest, so when "the season came" – harvest time – he sent his slave to collect "his share of the produce." But rather than honour their agreement, the tenants mistreat the slave and send him back to the owner with nothing. He then sends a series of slaves, first three in a row and then "many," but they, too, are mistreated and some are killed. The slaves represent the First Testament prophets, who were usually not well received by the Israelites when God first sent them. Matthew makes the point more explicit by specifying that one of the slaves is stoned (Matthew 21:35), matching Jesus' later description of Jerusalem as "the city that kills the prophets and stones those who are sent to it" (Matthew 23:37; cf. the stoning of the prophet Zechariah in 2 Chronicles 24:21).

The owner sends one last emissary, his "beloved son." This is obviously a reference to Jesus; in the Synoptic Gospels, the phrase "beloved son" is used only about Jesus. In fact, before this point in Mark's Gospel, Jesus has twice been called "the beloved" by God: at his baptism (1:11) and again at the Transfiguration (9:7). But rather than "respect" him, as the owner thinks they will, the tenants kill his "beloved son" and throw him out of the vineyard. This may be an allusion to efforts by the Jewish leaders (to whom the parable is addressed) to exclude Jesus and, after his death, his followers from the synagogue.

At this point, Jesus asks his audience what the owner will do in response to their treachery, and then provides his own answer. The owner will destroy the tenants and give the vineyard to others. This indicates that the Jewish leaders, by rejecting and ultimately killing Jesus, God's "beloved son," have forfeited their position as Israel's leaders; Jesus' disciples will replace them. It is not the vineyard itself, symbolizing Israel, that is rejected, but those who were supposed to look after it. There is no suggestion that Christianity has replaced Judaism; on the contrary, Christianity is presented as the continuation of the same vineyard that was planted in the First Testament (see Romans 11:17-24).

The parable itself ends there, but the Gospel writers have added two things. First, we find a quotation of Psalm 118:22-23: the "stone the builders rejected has become the cornerstone." This is meant to prove from the First Testament scriptures that despite the rejection of Jesus, God will use him as the foundation for the new community of Israel that God is building. Second, the Jewish leaders whom Jesus was addressing (see Mark 11:27) realized that the parable was about them and planned to arrest him, but did not do so because Jesus enjoyed great popularity among the people.

Since this parable is not about a general life situation but about Jesus' death, one might think that it has little direct relevance for us today. But it does contain some principles for the contemporary believer. First, God has great concern for the "vineyard." If we expand that concept of the vineyard to include all people of faith, regardless of their background, we will see that God cares greatly for the community (or communities) of faith, and that we should, too. Just as the owner showed great concern for his vineyard and expected it to produce quality grapes suitable for making wine, God expects us today to bear "good fruit." God also expects those to whom the vineyard has been entrusted to take care of it, not to abuse it or use it solely for their own benefit.

This leads us to a second point. We do not own the vineyard; we merely lease it from God. In other words, our faith communities do not belong to us, and certainly do not belong to our religious leaders. While our communities may have been entrusted to them, this is truly a matter of trust. God expects us to look after what belongs to God. And since the vineyard that is the community of faith covers the entire world, by extension this has implications for how we treat our world. We cannot simply exploit the planet for our own benefit, but must use it wisely for the benefit of all who live on it, now and in the future, knowing that eventually we must give it back to the Lord, to whom it belongs.

This parable also reminds us that God is patient. Two elements of the story reflect this. The first is the use of a vineyard as an image for God's people. Vines take at least three or four years to produce quality grapes. That means God does not demand an immediate return on this investment. Rather, God is willing to allow the vines time to develop. The series of envoys the vineyard owner sends to the tenants also reflects patience. The time span is not specified, but we can imagine it was substantial. God, too, has been patient with God's people. Finally, God sends his "beloved son," Jesus, to reveal God to us and call us to account. Even though some rejected him and some of us continue to do so, God has not yet evicted the tenants. But the parable tells us that the time will come when, like the vineyard owner, God's patience will run out and we will have to account for our stewardship of God's vineyard.

16

The Talents

"Well done, good and trustworthy slave."
Matthew 25:14-30

This parable deals with a man who entrusts various amounts of "talents" to three different slaves, "each according to his ability." This last phrase shows that this "talent" is not to be confused with the English meaning of a "gift" or "skill." The talents belong to the man, not the slaves, and since the first two slaves multiply them and then give them back along with the increase, this is not primarily an allegory about how we use our gifts. Although that does play a part in our eventual interpretation, the parable itself deals with financial matters.

As we saw in the parable of The Unmerciful Slave (Matthew 18:23-35; see Chapter 6 of this book), the talent was a unit of money that equalled about 6,000 days' wages for the average worker. The amounts of money involved, therefore, are substantial. The first two slaves use the talents they are given for trade, and are able to double the amounts in their care. The third one, however, buries the single talent he has been given. This was a fairly common practice for safekeeping in the ancient world: Matthew 13:44 compares God's reign to a treasure hidden in a field, and the Romans found valuables buried in a number of locations when they destroyed Jerusalem in 70 CE.

The master goes away for "a long time"; when he returns he summons the slaves to receive an account of how they have managed his money. The first steps forward and shows him the additional five talents he has earned from the five he was given. Likewise, the second gives his master four talents, twice the number he received. Both are praised and promised additional responsibilities in the future. The third slave, however, has no profit to offer his master. He explains that he was afraid of his master, whom he considers "a harsh man, reaping where you did not sow, and gathering where you did not scatter seed." Rather than risk failing to meet his master's expectations, he hid his talent in the ground to make sure he would at least be able to give it back when the time came.

The master gets angry, quoting the slave's own words back to him: since the slave knew that the master expected to receive something back from the work of others, he should at least have invested it. The interest it would have earned would not have increased the talent's value as much as the other two slaves did through trade, but at least it would have generated some profit. Therefore, the third slave is cast "into the outer darkness," in contrast to the first two, who are welcomed "into the joy of your master." The conclusion is obvious: the two who took risks and thereby benefited their master were rewarded, while the one who played it safe was punished.

In Matthew this parable is the second of three passages dealing with some aspect of Jesus' return and the Last Judgment. Immediately before this we find the parable of The Ten Bridesmaids (Matthew 25:1-12), who are waiting for the bridegroom (Jesus), who was delayed; immediately after it is a description of the Final Judgment in the parable of The Sheep and the Goats (Matthew 25:31-46; see Chapter 17 of this book). The master who goes away is clearly meant to represent Jesus after the Ascension. Although the master's absence was lengthy, that point is not emphasized and the slaves are not surprised when he eventually comes back. So the delay in Jesus' return is not the issue in this parable. Instead, the focus is on the fact that each slave is called to render an account of how he has handled the master's property while he was gone.

We noted above that this parable is not really about how we use our natural talents, but rather the story of a master calling his slaves to account for how they have handled different amounts of money. Nonetheless, when we consider the parable's meaning for Matthew's audience and for us, the former is a logical interpretation. In fact, the English nuance of the word "talent" as "ability" is based on this very passage. So, by extension, the parable teaches that we will all eventually be called to account for how we have used what God has given us: not sums of money, but abilities. And just like the master in the parable, a time will come when God will ask each of us how we have used those abilities for the benefit of the kingdom.

But there is more to this than a simple mathematical accounting. Each slave is given a different number of talents, "each according to his ability." Through this phrase Matthew recognizes the diversity of the Christian community, both then and now, as do other Second Testament writers. Paul, for instance, says, "we have gifts that differ according to the grace given to us" (Romans 12:6; cf. 1 Corinthians 12), while Ephesians 4:11-12 lists a variety of ministerial gifts that God has given to different members of the community "for building up the body of Christ."

This recognition that people have different abilities should both comfort and challenge us. For one thing, it frees us from having to do everything ourselves. This is good, because no one can do it all. Each person tends to be good at one or two things; together we have the gifts we need to build the kingdom of God. Recognizing that we have strengths but also weaknesses helps keep us humble and forces us to rely on others for the things we cannot do well. At the same time, we are inspired to serve within our own areas of strength for the good of the community. In this way we will live out Paul's teaching that, just as the various parts of the human body need each other in order to function as a whole, so too the Church depends on its members working together, each performing the functions that God enables them to do (1 Corinthians 12).

Another comforting aspect of the parable is that although the increase each slave brings to his master is different, both receive the same reward. The master addresses the exact same words to both: they are both promised authority over "many things" and told to "enter into the joy of your master." This means that our service of God is not a competition. God does not treat us according to how much we have done compared to others, but according to how much we have done compared to ourselves. We are to use our gifts for the greatest benefit of God and the community, and not worry about what someone else does with his or her abilities. As long as we offer all we have for the sake of others, we will receive the same reward.

But that introduces a challenge: we have to identify what our "talent" is; then we have to use it to the very best of our ability. What's more, we have to be willing to take risks. Remember that the first two slaves each doubled the amount of money they had been given. To double one's investment takes skill, but it also requires courage. There is always the potential for failure. The opposite approach is to follow the example of the third slave, who hid his money. Granted, it did not lose any of its value, but it gained nothing either, and therefore did not benefit the master or his household. In the same way, the kingdom of God is worth taking risks for, including the risk of falling short or even failing outright. That is part of what it means to have faith: being willing to take a chance in the belief that God will assist us.

In the end, each of us needs to decide what we have to offer for the sake of the kingdom. The first place to look is at our natural abilities, which come from God. God does not give us these gifts merely for our own benefit, but for the benefit of all. Eventually God will ask what we have done with those abilities. Our actions will determine whether we, too, hear those words of praise: "Well done, good and trustworthy slave."

17

The Sheep and the Goats

"Just as you did it to one of the least…
you did it to me."
Matthew 25:31-46

Strictly speaking, most of this passage does not qualify as a parable. Much of it is a straightforward description of Christ enthroned as a king at the Last Judgment. However, the division of humanity into two groups is compared to the action of a shepherd dividing his flock into sheep and goats. Furthermore, the image of the shepherd is rooted in a variety of First Testament texts that describe God as the Shepherd of Israel. In particular, Ezekiel 34:16 states that God will "feed [my sheep] with justice," and justice forms the basis on which the judgment is described here in Matthew. More directly, in Ezekiel 34:17, God says, "I shall judge between sheep and sheep, between rams and goats." So, although the comparison of Christ to a shepherd dividing his flock is a minor point in the passage itself, it does call to mind a well-established image for God and for God's actions.

Matthew's description of the Last Judgment is well known. When the Son of Man comes in glory he will be enthroned, surrounded by the angels and with all the nations before him. He will divide those assembled into two groups, represented as sheep and goats, on his right and left hand respectively. In the ancient world, one's right side was considered the place of honour, as reflected in Christ's position "at the right hand of the Father" in the Creed. Since most people are right-handed, that hand was used to bestow a blessing. Also, allowing someone to be on that side was a sign of trust: if I was on someone's right-hand side I could easily grab the person's right hand with my left, rendering him relatively defenceless, and then stab him with my right hand. We expect that those on Christ's right hand will be somehow honoured, and sure enough they are pronounced blessed and welcomed into the kingdom while the others are condemned to eternal punishment.

But note that Christ's judgment is not based on "religious" criteria. There is no mention made of the beliefs of the "sheep" or the "goats" or of the nature of their spiritual or ritual practices. Instead, the king concentrates on what they have done, and the action or inaction of each group is listed in identical terms. He notes whether they have fed him, given him something to drink, welcomed him, clothed him, nursed him when he was sick or visited him in prison. Both groups protest that they never saw him in any of those situations, and therefore cannot understand why they are either rewarded or condemned. To both groups Christ replies, "Just as you did [or did not do] it to the least of one of these who are members of my family, you did [or did not do] it to me."

In Matthew's Gospel "the least" are recipients of God's special concern. In particular, a series of texts in Matthew 18 single out the "little ones" as being especially deserving of attention. The greatest in the kingdom is identified as the little child (vv. 1-4), and those who welcome such children are said to welcome Jesus (v. 5). This is followed by a warning about causing one of the "little ones" to stumble (vv. 6-7) or despising them (v. 10), after which the parable of The Lost Sheep illustrates that "it is not the will of your Father in heaven that one of these little ones should be lost" (vv. 12-14; cf. Chapter 5 of this book). So this judgment scene builds upon what Jesus has said earlier in Matthew's Gospel, and especially on what he has said immediately before this in the chapter.

Matthew 18 builds on the notion of the covenant found in the First Testament. The covenant is a solemn agreement that binds God and the people together; it emphasizes that in order to be in a correct relationship with God, we must also be in a correct relationship with the other members of the covenant. But that is not all. God has repeatedly shown a special concern for the weakest members of society, starting with the liberation of a group of slaves from bondage in Egypt. From that point on, God takes the side of those who are neediest, what modern theologians and church leaders call having a "preferential option for the poor." Thus, a central aspect of God's plan for the world is that the weaker members of society, the "little ones," are to be provided for.

God's preferential option for the poor is illustrated here by the fact that Jesus identifies himself with the hungry, the naked, the thirsty, the sick and the imprisoned. That is why the people in the Last Judgment are rewarded or punished on the basis of how they treated such people in their midst. This approach has profound implications for how we can and should understand our relationship with God. The most immediate way we can relate to God is by responding to the needs of those with whom God identifies the most. It is worth noting again that at no point in the passage is there any reference to the beliefs of either group, the "sheep" or the "goats." For instance, the Lord does not ask whether they could explain the doctrine of the Trinity or recite the Creed. What matters is not what they believe but what they have done. Their attentiveness to the needs of "the least" determines their admission into eternal punishment or into eternal life.

Something else that the parable emphasizes, though, is that neither group acted as they did because they consciously saw (or failed to see) Christ in the people around them. They both ask, "When was it that we saw you?" Their actions are the result of automatic responses to the needy that spring from the overall orientation of their lives.

Even the "sheep" are amazed that through their actions they were ministering to Christ.

Our overall orientation does not come into existence all at once, or in response to a specific situation. By its very nature, it is the result of how we live. Our basic orientation, be it selfish or giving, will be revealed in our attitude towards others. When we met someone in need, we will usually respond from this orientation. If we tend to help others then we will help this time, but if we tend not to help others then we will not help this time. If our tendency is not to help, we may make excuses for not helping, but we probably will not wonder whether this is one of the "least" with whom Jesus identifies.

This does not mean we cannot change, however. Since the basic orientation of our life is determined by how we usually act, if we change how we usually act then we can change our orientation. If necessary, reminding ourselves of this passage might help us to do so. At first, we might need to ask consciously whether those we meet in our lives are the "least" about whom Jesus speaks in order to change how we respond. But before long, a different response in a series of individual situations will bring about a change in our overall orientation. When that happens, we will act less because we are thinking of the sheep and goats and more because we are motivated by the love of others, especially the love for the weaker members of society that God desires each of us to have.

All of us can benefit from thinking from time to time about who constitutes the "least" among us. The types of people Jesus mentions are not meant to be a complete list, since God's love can never be exhausted. God is always seeking new people to receive that love, and uses us to channel it to them. Our society and culture have changed since the time of Jesus, so it is important to consider what other groups we can add to the list. Surely that concern is not limited to the hungry, the naked, the thirsty, the sick and the imprisoned. The common characteristic of those groups is that they are in need, and the people today who fit that description are many. Indeed, all of us are needy in some way.

The lesson we learn from this text is clear: it is not what we believe or proclaim that is ultimately important, but how we live. As we saw in Chapter 1 of this book, Jesus says the same thing elsewhere in the Gospel: "Not every one who says to me, 'Lord, Lord,' shall enter the kingdom of heaven, but only the one who does the will of my Father in heaven" (Matthew 7:21). Jesus calls all of us to do the will of his (and our) Father, beginning now with those around us who are in need. Whether we realize it or not, we will be doing it to, and for, him.

Index of Scripture References

Genesis
4:23-24   50
31:39   41

Exodus
20:12   72
22:10-13   41

Leviticus
16:29-34   90
19:18   56
21:1-3   57
21:11   57
23:27-32   90
27:30-33   90

Numbers
5:2   57
18:20-32   90
19:11-20   57
19:16   57
29:7   90

Deuteronomy
5:16   72
6:5   56
14:22-27   90

25:17-18   83
26:2-13   90

1 Kings
22:17   42

2 Kings
9:7   68
17:24-34   55

2 Chronicles
24:21   104

Ezra
4:1-3   55
9:11   68

Psalms
14:1   61
77:20   41
104:16-17   37
118:22-23   105
123:1   91

Proverbs
24:16   50

Qoheleth (Ecclesiastes)
5:13-14   60
6:1-6   60

Sirach (Ecclesiasticus)
11:18   60
11:19   60
14:3-10   60
50:25-26   55

Isaiah
5:1-2   103
5:1-7   94, 102
17:1-11   31
27:2-6   94, 102
40:11   41
53:6   42
55:8-9   98

Jeremiah
5:28   84
7:25   68
12:10   94, 102
23:1-4   42
50:6   42
51:33   31

Ezekiel
17:22-23   37
31:6   37
34:4   42

34:6   42
34:11   42
34:16   114
34:17   114
38:17   68
44:25-27   57

Amos
1–2   25
3:7   68
3:12   41

Daniel
4:20-21   37
9:6   68

Zechariah
1:6   68
7:9-10   84

Matthew
5-7   17
5:39   18-19
5:41   18
7:21   20, 119
7:24-27   15-21
9:37-38   31
10:5   55
13:24-30   29-34, 68
13:31   35
13:36-43   30

13:37-40	30, 31
13:44	109
16:18	43
17:20	36
18	116
18:5	116
18:6-7	116
18:10	116
18:10-14	40-46
18:12-14	116
18:15	43
18:15-17	44
18:17	43
18:21-22	44
18:23-35	44, 47-52, 108
20:1-16	94-100, 102
21:28-32	94, 102
21:35	104
22:1-10	64-70
23:37	68, 104
25:1-12	110
25:14-30	108-113
25:31-46	110, 114-119

Mark

1:11	104
1:15	17-18
4:1-9	22-28
4:8	24
4:9	26

4:14	26
4:13-20	25
4:30-32	35-39
9:7	104
11:27	105
12:1-9	94, 101-107

Luke

6:46	19
7:11-17	83
9:51-56	55
10:25-37	53-58
12:16-21	59-63
12:15	61
12:33	62
13:6	102
13:19	35
14:7-10	65
14:16-24	64-70
15:1-7	40-46, 76
15:8-10	76
15:11-32	71-76
16:1-8	77-81
17:6	36
18:1-8	82-86
18:9-14	87-93
18:22	62
18:25	63
20:45–21:4	83

John
1:46   27
4:9   55
11:41   91

Romans
11:17-24   105
12:6   111

1 Corinthians
3:4-6   33
12   111, 112

1 Thessalonians
4:15   85
4:17   85

Ephesians
4:11-12   111

1 Timothy
2:8   91

Also available from Novalis

The Questions of Jesus

Miracles of Jesus

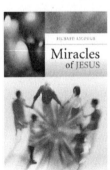

Available in 2005
Teachings of Jesus

For these and other
fine books, contact
NOVALIS
1-800-387-7164
or
cservice@novalis.ca

Visit our web site:
www.novalis.ca

AGMV Marquis

MEMBRE DE SCABRINI MEDIA

Québec, Canada
2004